Current
CONTROVERSIES

Healthcare

Other books in the Current Controversies series

Alcoholism

Alternative Energy Sources

Cancer

Child Abuse

Conserving the Environment

The Elderly

Hate Crimes

Sexual Harassment

Suicide

Teenage Pregnancy and Parenting

Weapons of Mass Destruction

Healthcare

Jan Grover, Book Editor

GREENHAVEN PRESS

An imprint of Thomson Gale, a part of The Thomson Corporation

Detroit • New York • San Francisco • New Haven, Conn. • Waterville, Maine • London

Christine Nasso, *Publisher*
Elizabeth Des Chenes, *Managing Editor*

© 2007 Thomson Gale, a part of The Thomson Corporation.

Thomson and Star logo are trademarks and Gale and Greenhaven Press are registered trademarks used herein under license.

For more information, contact:
Greenhaven Press
27500 Drake Rd.
Farmington Hills, MI 48331-3535
Or you can visit our Internet site at http://www.gale.com

Articles in Greenhaven Press anthologies are often edited for length to meet page requirements. In addition, original titles of these works are changed to clearly present the main thesis and to explicitly indicate the author's opinion. Every effort is made to ensure that Greenhaven Press accurately reflects the original intent of the authors. Every effort has been made to trace the owners of copyrighted material.

LIBRARY OF CONGRESS CATALOGING-IN-PUBLICATION DATA

Healthcare / Jan Grover, book editor.
  p. cm. -- (Current controversies)
  Includes bibliographical references and index.
  ISBN-13: 978-0-7377-3427-0 (hardcover)
  ISBN-10: 0-7377-3427-2 (hardcover)
  ISBN-13: 978-0-7377-3428-7 (pbk.)
  ISBN-10: 0-7377-3428-0 (pbk.)
  1. Medical care--Juvenile literature. 2. Social medicine--Juvenile literature.
  3. Health--Juvenile literature. I. Grover, Jan
  RA777.H4354 2007
  362.1--dc22
                                                                2006038690

Printed in the United States of America
10 9 8 7 6 5 4 3 2 1

Contents

Foreword   13

Introduction   16

Chapter 1: Should Healthcare Be Considered a Basic Right?

Chapter Preface   21

Yes: Healthcare Is a Basic Right

The Basic Right to Health Care   23
Is the Unfinished Business of the
United States Government

Jean Camalt and Sarah Zaidi

President Franklin Roosevelt proposed a "Second Bill of Rights" in 1943 that included the right to medical care. This unfinished business of government needs to be addressed now.

The United States Should Guarantee   27
the Right to Health Care through
a Constitutional Amendment

Jesse L. Jackson Jr.

A Constitutional amendment would ensure that all citizens of the United States have equal rights to high-quality health care and the right to sue government if it is not provided.

Access to Health Care: A Right, Not   32
a Privilege

Tom Harkin

Health care—not just treatment for disease but access to preventive treatment—should be a right. All Americans should have access to the same coverage as federal employees do.

No: Healthcare Is Not a Human Right

No "Right" to Health Care Exists   35

Wayne Dunn

Real rights don't impose the needs of some on everyone else—taxpayers, physicians, and institutions.

Bogus Rights   **38**
Walter E. Williams

Rights involve takings by Congress, and already three-fifths to two-thirds of the federal budget involves transfers of property from one citizen to another. Medical rights, like food and housing, are not guaranteed by Congress or upheld by the Constitution.

Even Nations with Health Care Rights   **41**
Are Moving Away from Universal Care
David Gratzer

In a landmark 2005 decision, the Canadian Supreme Court ruled that citizens can opt out of Canada's universal health-care system and buy private coverage.

Chapter 2: Can the Existing American Healthcare System Be Saved?

Chapter Preface   **46**

Yes: Market-Driven Reforms Can Save the System

The Problem with the Health Care System Is   **48**
Not Health Care But America's Tax Code
R. Glenn Hubbard

America has adequate health care resources, but its tax code fails to reward personal responsibility and to remove impediments to private markets, two moves that would save the system.

Eliminating Excessive Regulations Can Cure   **53**
America's Health Care System
Scott W. Atlas

Government regulations raise the cost of health care for everyone. Eliminate the artificial pricing structure caused by excessive regulation, and the market for health care can regulate itself to consumers' advantage.

Medical Bankruptcy Is an Overblown Threat;   56
Most People with High Medical Bills Are
Covered by Insurance
    Gail Heriot

    Thanks to a market-driven system in which the average
    patient pays only $1,100 in out-of-pocket expenses for
    high medical bills, few Americans with high medical bills
    have to file for medical bankruptcy.

**No: America's Existing Healthcare System
Cannot Be Repaired**

Our Existing Health Care System Has Failed   61
to Contain Sky-Rocketing Health Care Costs
    Paul B. Ginsburg and Cara S. Lesser

    Managed care was supposed to be the salvation of
    America's health care system. Instead, it has widened the
    disparity between health care "haves" and "have nots."

America's Current System of Health Care   72
Endangers Patients and Providers
    Mehmet Oz

    Erratic insurance coverage, balkanized patient records,
    and the threat of malpractice suits leave America's exist-
    ing health care system inadequate for patients and physi-
    cians alike.

**Chapter 3: How Should Healthcare
Be Reformed?**

Chapter Preface   78
    Consumer-Driven Health Care Can Solve
    America's Health Care Problems

Consumer-Driven Health Care Prompts   81
People to Spend Less on Health Care
    Devon M. Herrick

    People can now manage their own care through e-mail,
    self-administered tests, the Internet, and other new meth-
    ods, thus keeping medical expenses down. Deregulating
    health care can extend these new approaches to more
    consumers.

High-Deductible Health Plans Bring Down   96
Insurance Costs for Consumers
  Scott W. Atlas

  Raising health insurance deductibles makes insurance
  more affordable, eliminates small claims, and reduces administrative costs.

Thorough Privatization Will Provide   100
Needed Reforms
  John C. Goodman

  Increasing patient power through tax reform, Health Savings Accounts, insurance portability, and nationally available health plans should be the focus in solving America's
  health-care problems.

Deregulating Health Care Can Make Services   106
More Affordable
  Christopher J. Conover

  Health services regulations amount to 8.9 percent of
  health-care costs. Deregulation could keep more dollars
  in consumers' hands and thus improve their health and
  security.

Medicaid Should Be Restructured So   111
the Poorest and Weakest Can Buy Whatever
Health Care They Choose
  Jeffrey M. Jones

  Hurricane Katrina (2005) shed light on the many weak-
  nesses of Medicaid as a program for providing health
  care for the poor. The marketplace can handle these services more effectively than the federal program.

**No: Consumer-Driven Health Plans Cannot Solve
America's Healthcare Problems**

Consumer-Driven Health Plans Are   120
Not Effective
  Paul Fronstin and Sara R. Collins

  Studies of high-deductible and consumer-driven health
  plans reveal that people are less satisfied, spend more,
  and defer more health care than people using other forms
  of health insurance.

Consumer-Driven Health Plans Erode Health   123
Care for All Americans
Paul Krugman and Robin Wells

Consumer-driven health plans are tax breaks for the
wealthy, undermine employment-based health care, ignore evidence that they worsen health care for most
people, both those who use them and those who don't.

Consumer-Driven Health Care Will Not   129
Eliminate the High Costs of Private Care
Hendrik Hertzberg

The Bush administration's drive to further privatize
health care ignores the high administrative and technology costs of medical care and focuses instead on blaming
consumers for high health-care costs.

Consumer-Driven Health Plans Do Not   134
Provide Equal and Sufficient Information for
Making Informed Medical Decisions
Cheryl Damberg

Consumer-driven health plans (CDHPs) are new and un-
tested. Studies over the last 5 to 7 years indicate that
consumers of CDHPs have unequal access and ability to
make their own health-management decisions.

Market Models Do not Apply to America's   142
Current Health Care Crisis
David R. Francis

Medical care is not a market commodity, so market incentives and practices cannot keep prices down and provide comprehensive coverage.

Leaving Medicaid to the Market Has   146
Destroyed the Program in Tennessee
Trudy Lieberman

TennCare, the state of Tennessee's once-model Medicaid
program, has been gutted by deregulation and market
"management." As a result, thousands of previously enrolled low-income citizens have lost their health coverage.

Chapter 4: How Should America's Healthcare System Be Transformed?

Chapter Preface   156
    The United States Should Move Toward More Personal
    Responsibility for Health Care

Government's Involvement in Health Care   158
Should Reward Individual Responsibility
    Michael F. Cannon
    Government involvement in America's health-care system
    discourages individual responsibility and encourages
    overspending.

True Health-Care Reform Must Return   160
Decision Making to Individuals
    *Robert E. Moffit, Grace V. Smith, and
    Jennifer A. Marshall*
    The role of government in health care should be to pro-
    tect Americans' basic freedom to choose treatment com-
    patible with their values and their individual choices.

Health Care Should Be a   165
Personal Responsibility
    Radley Balko
    Increasingly, government is invading the arena of per-
    sonal choice when it comes to individual health. The best
    public approach to health care is the approach that maxi-
    mizes the personal freedom of citizens to make their own
    health-care decisions.

Health Insurance and "Personal   169
Responsibility": Shifting the Bill from
the Employer to the Worker
    Judi King
    Efforts by conservative politicians would shift the burden
    of responsibility for health-care coverage from employ-
    ers, where most of it now resides, to individuals, worsen-
    ing our health-care crisis.

A Single-Payer System Will Be Good for **176**
American Business

Morton Minz

Publicly financed health care will cost employers less in
taxes than their current costs for insurance while extending health care to everyone.

Let's Provide Medicare for All Americans **184**

Pete Stark

By extending the federal government's already successful
Medicare program for the elderly and disabled, America
can create universal coverage at a proven lower cost than
private insurance.

Glossary **186**

Organizations to Contact **191**

Bibliography **200**

Index **206**

Foreword

By definition, controversies are "discussions of questions in which opposing opinions clash" (Webster's Twentieth Century Dictionary Unabridged). Few would deny that controversies are a pervasive part of the human condition and exist on virtually every level of human enterprise. Controversies transpire between individuals and among groups, within nations and between nations. Controversies supply the grist necessary for progress by providing challenges and challengers to the status quo. They also create atmospheres where strife and warfare can flourish. A world without controversies would be a peaceful world; but it also would be, by and large, static and prosaic.

The Series' Purpose

The purpose of the Current Controversies series is to explore many of the social, political, and economic controversies dominating the national and international scenes today. Titles selected for inclusion in the series are highly focused and specific. For example, from the larger category of criminal justice, Current Controversies deals with specific topics such as police brutality, gun control, white collar crime, and others. The debates in Current Controversies also are presented in a useful, timeless fashion. Articles and book excerpts included in each title are selected if they contribute valuable, long-range ideas to the overall debate. And wherever possible, current information is enhanced with historical documents and other relevant materials. Thus, while individual titles are current in focus, every effort is made to ensure that they will not become quickly outdated. Books in the Current Controversies series will remain important resources for librarians, teachers, and students for many years.

In addition to keeping the titles focused and specific, great care is taken in the editorial format of each book in the series. Book introductions and chapter prefaces are offered to provide background material for readers. Chapters are organized around several key questions that are answered with diverse opinions representing all points on the political spectrum. Materials in each chapter include opinions in which authors clearly disagree as well as alternative opinions in which authors may agree on a broader issue but disagree on the possible solutions. In this way, the content of each volume in Current Controversies mirrors the mosaic of opinions encountered in society. Readers will quickly realize that there are many viable answers to these complex issues. By questioning each author's conclusions, students and casual readers can begin to develop the critical thinking skills so important to evaluating opinionated material.

Current Controversies is also ideal for controlled research. Each anthology in the series is composed of primary sources taken from a wide gamut of informational categories including periodicals, newspapers, books, U.S. and foreign government documents, and the publications of private and public organizations. Readers will find factual support for reports, debates, and research papers covering all areas of important issues. In addition, an annotated table of contents, an index, a book and periodical bibliography, and a list of organizations to contact are included in each book to expedite further research.

Perhaps more than ever before in history, people are confronted with diverse and contradictory information. During the Persian Gulf War, for example, the public was not only treated to minute-to-minute coverage of the war, it was also inundated with critiques of the coverage and countless analyses of the factors motivating U.S. involvement. Being able to sort through the plethora of opinions accompanying today's major issues, and to draw one's own conclusions, can be a complicated and frustrating struggle. It is the editors' hope that Current Controversies will help readers with this struggle.

Introduction

*"The United States is the only industrial-
ized nation that lacks a countrywide system of government-provided or
-subsidized health insurance for all its
citizens."*

Health care is emerging as one of the biggest issues in
American employment and family life. To put it in perspective, consider this: according to a 2005 RAND Corporation health-care study, the American family in 2004 was paying an average of $2,661 for its share of employer-provided
health insurance; the American employer, an average of $7,289
for each employee's family coverage. These rates rose by 10
percent in the single year 2003–2004. The average annual increase in cost of personal health-care expenditures between
1980 and 2004 has been 8.6 percent; as a portion of U.S. gross
domestic product, health care consumed 15 percent of all the
dollars made in 2004. Consumer surveys conducted by the
federal government in 1996 and 2003 and reported in 2006 in
the *Journal of the American Medical Association* found that almost 50 million Americans below the age of 65 (when federal
Medicare insurance becomes available to all citizens) were
paying more than 10 percent of their family incomes on health
care costs.

Such high costs vastly increase the amount that families,
individuals, and businesses must earn to meet their needs.
They greatly increase the operating costs of businesses, government, and not-for-profit organizations. They make the cost
of goods and services produced by American businesses significantly higher than those produced by businesses in other
industrialized countries, where the cost of medical insurance
is borne by the government—for example, General Motors

pays an average of $1,500 per vehicle built in the United States in employees' health-care costs, while General Motors in Canada pays about $500. Such differences in built-in costs are increasingly making American products uncompetitive in global markets.

The United States is the only industrialized nation that lacks a countrywide system of government-provided or -subsidized health insurance for all its citizens. For most of this country's history, most people paid hospitals, physicians, and other health-care providers directly for medical services. Early exceptions to this were insurance plans sold to lumberjacks and other workers; in the late nineteenth and early twentieth centuries, such workers would contribute a dime, a quarter, or fifty cents each time they were paid to ensure that their medical care would be provided in the event of sickness or accident. As workers' unions formed across the country, they began providing medical benefits for their members. During worker shortages on the homefront in World War II—most men of draft age were serving in the armed forces—some employers, unable to increase wages because of restrictions imposed by the federal government, began to offer medical insurance to employees in lieu of raising employees' pay. Following World War II, these programs stayed in place; employers became the source for ensuring that most Americans' medical expenses were met.

This is no longer the case. Because health insurance has become so expensive, fewer large employers are now offering it to employees—64 percent in 1999, 60 percent in 2004, the latest year for which records are available, and far less for small employers—and many employees can no longer afford to pay their increasingly larger share of monthly premiums. Today, one-third of all Americans lack health insurance at least part of each year. The most underinsured age group is young adults aged 18 to 24: because many in this age group work part-time or for small companies, 30 percent entirely lack health insurance. The cost per person of health care annually now averages $5,267 in the United States—50 percent more than the next-highest-spending nation, Switzerland, spends. Yet the United States stands only thirty-sixth in infant mortality rate and twenty-ninth in average life expectancy. Clearly, despite America's great expenditures on health care, citizens here are not getting as much for their money as citizens in other industrialized countries, nor are as many U.S. citizens getting coverage of any kind, compared to those in other industrialized countries.

Medical Expenses

Only thirty years ago, the range of available tests and treatments was far smaller than it is today. The growing use of costly equipment, such as magnetic resonance imaging (MRI) and computerized tomography (CT) scans, accounts for one of the chief factors in rising medical expenses. As competing health maintenance organizations (HMOs) and other providers attempt to attract and keep paying patients, each builds up its own elaborate system of equipment, testing, therapy, hospital, outpatient-clinic, and hospice care, the end results of which are duplication of costly goods and services. These, in turn, are passed on to employers and consumers in the form of higher health insurance costs and deductibles.

Other factors enter into the United States' steadily mounting health-care costs: government-mandated staff-to-patient ratios and mandated policies; state-mandated coverage of certain tests and preventive measures for all residents, no matter their form of health coverage; costs associated with court-awarded claims for malpractice and claims against faulty equipment; administrative costs, as each health plan staffs its own claims, benefits, and case management. Where liberal, conservative, and libertarian policy analysts and critics differ is in the weight they assign to each of these observable causes of steadily rising health-care costs.

As you will discover while reading the selections in this volume, none of its contributors—and these range from physicians in private and corporate practice to think-tank theorists to federal policy makers to congressional legislators to media pundits—agree on which factors are of greatest importance. Nor do they agree on what the solutions to the undeniable crisis in American health care are: some stress legislative action; others, business initiatives; others, consumer action; others, the action of attorneys and the judiciary.

What is certain is that the cost of American health care is reaching the breaking point for employers and employees in the private sector, for federal and state governments, and for individuals caught between these various systems.

Should Healthcare Be Considered a Basic Right?

Chapter Preface

No issue surrounding U.S. health care is more basic or contentious than that of whether or not health care is a human right. European countries have long regarded it as such; this understanding is reflected in the European Union's Charter of Fundamental Rights (2000). It was incorporated into the United Nations' Universal Declaration of Human Rights in 1948. Within both of America's nearest neighboring countries, Mexico and Canada, health care is regarded as a citizen's right and the government's responsibility.

Our nation's history is different from other nations', so it is perhaps not surprising that the United States, unlike other industrialized countries, has not implemented a universal, government-provided health-care system. It is worth remembering that our government is a federated system of fifty semi-independent states, and that most health-care regulation is carried out by those states rather than by the federal government. Some states provide government-funded health care to citizens who cannot otherwise find affordable insurance, thus putting those governments in a role similar to that played by the National Health Service in Canada. In more states than not, however, government provides health care only for indigent citizens through Medicaid, a jointly funded and administered, state and federal program. Otherwise, access to health care is a private matter between citizen and employer or citizen and insurance company.

Unlike a great many other issues involving the health-care industry, health care as a basic human right seems to divide politicians, voters, and policy makers into only two camps: those who believe it is a right and those who believe that it is not. The liberal positions you will find in this chapter argue for visions of health care that range from those claiming that government is morally obliged to provide medical treatment to all U.S. residents to others that view the right to health care as including equal access to decent housing and decent food. Government, liberals contend, should be used to improve citizens' lives—and what could have a greater impact on people's happiness and productivity than adequate medical care? Because government could keep the significant (and growing) administrative costs of America's current patchwork of health-care systems lower than the many different corporations now administering benefits, scrutinizing applications, and managing care, liberals favor a single-payer system; they claim that it would keep costs down and make access more equitable. Liberals believe that government regulation is necessary to prevent health care from becoming just another industry in which market values—vertical integration, elimination of competition, selective denial of services, and deregulation—supersede those of fairness and universality.

Libertarians and conservatives, on the other hand, do not consider health care, or access to it, as a basic human right. While many of them deplore the limited access to care that America's present system of health care has produced, they favor market solutions to eliminate these inequities. Health care, they believe, is a service industry, and like other industries, it is regulated, funded, and administered most effectively by private enterprise. They point to the economies of scale made possible by deregulating the industry, the possibility of lower costs through competition, and the history of privately funded innovation that has made America's technologically advanced medicine respected throughout the world.

It is striking that no middle ground exists in this debate, unlike others in this volume. While lively exchanges about the *how* of providing expanded access to health care occur among liberals, libertarians, and conservatives, no such dialogue occurs between those who view access to health care as an irreducible human right and those who see it as a service purchased like any other.

The Basic Right to Health Care Is the Unfinished Business of the United States Government

Jean Camalt and Sarah Zaidi

About the author*: Jean Camalt is the legal coordinator for the Center for Economic and Social Rights (CESR), an organization promoting social justice through human rights. Sarah Zaidi is the director and cofounder of CESR. Her most recent work has addressed conflict and economic and social rights.*

In 1941, President Franklin D. Roosevelt proclaimed "freedom from want" to be one of the four essential liberties necessary to achieve human security. The four freedoms include freedom of speech, freedom of religion, freedom from want, and freedom from fear. Roosevelt's "Second Bill of Rights" also included the right to work, the right to earn enough for adequate food, clothing, and recreation, the right of farmers and businessmen to fair business practices, markets, and trade, the right to housing, the right to economic security, and the right to education. The polio-stricken President included in his definition of freedom "the right to adequate medical care and the opportunity to achieve and enjoy good health." This right to health was subsequently included in the Universal Declaration of Human Rights, drafted with American guidance, and has since been enshrined in many international and regional human rights treaties. [This resolution was adopted and proclaimed by the new organization the United Nations in 1948.]

Jean Camalt and Sarah Zaidi, "Introduction," Center for Economic and Social Rights/ cesr.org, October 2004. Reproduced by permission.

A Promise Unfulfilled

In the U.S. today, this freedom remains unrealized. Forty-four million Americans lack health insurance completely. A full third of Americans live without health care for at least part of the year. And the quality of health care for all but the wealthiest patients has declined dramatically, with more people dying each year from avoidable medical mistakes than from car accidents. Add to these problems the lack of services for Americans in rural areas, discrimination in health care provision and outcomes between whites and non-white minorities, and pharmaceutical and insurance costs that are spiraling out of control, and it is clear the U.S. health care system is in profound crisis.

The U.S. healthcare system has reached a point where critical and dramatic action is needed.

How is this possible when the United States spends more per person on health care than any other industrialized country in the world? The health care crisis in this country is more complex than questions of rising costs or lack of insurance, and as important as those elements may be, any successful reform of the health care system must take a broader approach to understanding the problems.

Health Care as a Human Right

Can an international human rights framework offer anything new to the debate over the American health care crisis? We believe that it can. Posing the familiar problems with the U.S. health care system as matters of fundamental rights opens a space for new solutions to problems that currently result in certain people and social groups being systematically harmed by the government's inaction, as well as by its failure to regulate others' actions. International human rights norms provide standards by which to evaluate a government's conduct and can be used to articulate demands for accountability. Acknowledging a *right* to health can shift policy debates from a narrow focus on "efficiency" (itself a spurious notion when many costs—e.g., the loss of productivity due to employee health problems—are simply "externalized") to questions of how to guarantee people an effective voice in policy and programming decisions that affect their well-being. [By "externalized," the authors mean that the actual costs of a problem—in this case, health care—are not accounted for and instead seen as outside the problem.]

Mobilizing Support for Universal Health Care

Traditional approaches to human rights violations have often focused on legislative reform. Yet, the human rights movement has also been an effective instrument for mobilizing grassroots political support for substantial policy, as well as legislative, changes. The U.S. health care system has reached a point where critical and dramatic action is needed, which in turn requires the kind of popular support created by a rights-based campaign. A human rights framework offers a path forward for those who advocate major changes to the system which would restore *health* to its proper place at the center of health care legislation, policies, and practice.

This will be a long and difficult struggle. The United States government has historically resisted guarantees of social and economic rights, and has refused to ratify international and regional legal instruments intended to ensure these rights. Despite President Roosevelt's vision of a Second Bill of Rights, and his leadership in establishing an international system with the United Nations at its center, the U.S. has a poor record of implementing international human rights standards on the domestic level. Moreover, the legacy of Cold War propaganda persists as an obstacle to health care reform, as corporation and conservative pundits continue to suggest that government involvement [with] the health care system would constitute "socialized medicine." Health care, they argue, is a commodity, and those health guarantees that do exist in the U.S., generally at the state level, should best be thought of [as] charity, rather than as legally enforceable obligations.

The United States Should Guarantee the Right to Health Care Through a Constitutional Amendment

Jesse L. Jackson Jr.

About the author: *Jesse L. Jackson Jr. is a member of the United States House of Representatives from Illinois. He is a Democrat and the son of Jesse Jackson, the civil rights activist and several-times candidate for the presidency of the United States.*

What idea do I have to *insure* that all Americans will have high quality health care? I'm proposing to add a health care amendment to the U.S. Constitution! . . .

The proposed amendment is House Joint Resolution 30.

H. J. Res. 30, states:

Section 1. All citizens of the United States shall enjoy the right to health care of equal high quality.

Section 2. The Congress shall have power to implement this article by appropriate legislation.

Constitutional amendments are broad statements of principle that establish a premise, a foundation and framework—or in this instance a right—upon which legislation must be built. Congress, through the laws it passes, and in the final analysis the court's interpretation of those laws, will define the amendment's meaning at any given time in American history.

In constitutional amendments, every idea, concept and word is important. So let's examine H.J. Res. 30.

Jesse L. Jackson Jr., "A Health Care Constitutional Amendment: Its Meaning and Implications," in www.house.gov/apps/list/speech/il02_jackson/041209HealthCareAmend .html, April 27, 2005.

What Constitutionally Guaranteed Health Care Means

1. Like the first ten amendments to the Constitution—the Bill of Rights—this amendment provides every American with an *individual* right.

2. It's an individual right that is *universal*—it applies to "all citizens" of the United States. It's the only absolute 100 percent solution to our health care dilemma and crisis! It's the only proposal that actually and in reality covers everyone and "leaves no American behind." No other plan, Democratic or Republican, guarantees that every American will have a right to high quality health care.

3. H.J. Res. 30 uses the terms "shall enjoy." That means it's a positive and affirmative individual right as well as a societal and governmental obligation. Most current amendments to the Constitution are legitimate *limitations* on the government and provide individual protection from the government. They tell you what government cannot do. Government can't interfere with your right to free speech, your right to peaceably assembly and protest, your right to privacy, and your right to engage in the religion of your choice or to choose to practice no religion at all.

4. H.J. Res. 30 puts "the right to health care" in the Constitution. It means the human and moral right to health care would become a *legal right* that can be realized through legislation and enforced in a court of law. The Constitution would be affirming that every individual American is entitled to health care—that health care, like free speech and freedom of religion, is a new American citizenship right.

5. The amendment says that every American is entitled to health care "of equal high quality." The amendment doesn't merely say "equal," because "equal" could lead to

a "zero-sum" outcome—that is, lowering the highest standards and raising the lowest standards to meet in some amorphous middle. That would satisfy no one. The standard in this amendment is "equal *high* quality," which means that every American would be entitled to the best health care the American economy, the medical profession, and the health care system can provide. As the economy grows stronger and medical science advances, all of the American people would benefit—to the degree possible and on a continuous basis, and for as long as the country and the Constitution exist.

6. The second part of the amendment assigns Congress the *power* and the *affirmative responsibility* to write legislation that will provide every American with health care of equal high quality. Without the amendment, no member of Congress has a legal mandate to draft or fund universal health care legislation, and no court has a constitutional basis to enforce any comprehensive health, care plan that is offered by Congress, whether Medical Savings Accounts, single-payer or something else. . . .

How Can America Afford Universal Coverage?

"Can we afford such a right"? Some respond, "Morally, we can't afford not to have such a right."

Let me try to combine both questions in my answer.

There is no question that our $11 trillion economy is the largest and strongest in the world. It dwarfs every other nation. On the other hand, we are the only industrialized democracy that doesn't have a national health care system for all of its citizens—other than the most expensive last resort of an emergency room. The only citizens who are legally guaranteed a right to health care are prisoners.

It's not logical that we boast the most advanced and powerful internationally integrated economy in the world, then claim

*organizational incompetence and poverty when it comes to cre-
ating and funding a national health care system for all Americans.*

Additionally, we spend a lot more money on health care
than any other nation, approximately 15 percent of our Gross
Domestic Product (GDP) or about $1.7 trillion. With much
smaller economics, Canada spends around 9 percent and other
nation's significantly less—but they cover all of their citizens.
It's why, according to the World Health Organization (WHO),
we barely rank in the top 50 nations in the world (37th) in
terms of meeting the health care needs of our people. In part,
it's because about 25 percent of our health expenditures have
nothing to do with providing health care. One-quarter of our
private health dollars are spent on advertising, bureaucracy
and other, non-health-care-related activities—compared to 2-3
percent for Medicare. If we spent the same amount of money
(currently $1.7 trillion or 15% of our GDP) more efficiently
and effectively, and created a unique American health care system on the basis of H.J. Res. 30, we would have the greatest
health care system ever constructed for all of the American
people.

---

*Putting a new health care right in the Constitution would
be morally, economically and physically beneficial to the
nation.*

In short, we have the best health care system in the world
for those who have the money to pay for it. But 44 million
(and growing) Americans have no health insurance, and 49
million in the middle class are becoming dissatisfied with the
health insurance they have, because it is growing ever more
expensive even as it is providing fewer services and less care.

The truth is, health care is not a national priority, and our
health care system is not efficiently or effectively organized. . . .

A constitutional rights approach would repair and modernize aging hospitals, build thousands of new hospitals, rehabilitation centers, community health clinics, nursing homes, and hospice care facilities—which would mean jobs for bricklayers, plasterers, carpenters, electricians, glaziers, roofers and brick masons.

We would have to equip these facilities with sophisticated medical equipment, beds, bedpans, tables, chairs, surgical gloves, sheets, pillows and much more—a huge boost in money and jobs for those businesses that produce and supply health care goods and services.

We would need to train thousands of health professionals, including doctors, nurses, paramedics, nurses' aids, home care workers and others who provide health care—not to mention the thousands of basic workers who scrub and wax the floors, clean the other public areas, cut the grass, shovel the snow, and in many other ways physically maintain our health facilities.

As a result of this health care amendment, we would create a surplus of health care and other professionals. Thus, instead of exporting wars and weapons of mass destruction—the U.S. sells one-half of all military weapons sold in the world—we would be exporting builders of hospitals, health administrators, doctors, nurses, medical care, and training indigenous people in other nations to become healing agents themselves. . . .

Thus, putting a new health care right in the Constitution would be morally, economically and physically beneficial to the nation. It would be a permanent and universal fix for the nation's health care needs, while at the same time aid in providing employment and economic stimulus, stability and security.

Access to Health Care: A Right, Not a Privilege

Tom Harkin

About the author: *Tom Harkin is a Democrat and United States senator from Iowa. He has served in Congress since 1974. He is cochair of the Senate Rural Health Caucus and has been interested in health-care issues since childhood because of his brother's lifelong disability.*

Something is wrong when 45 million Americans—eight out of 10 of them in working families—can't afford even basic health insurance. . . .

Without the Right to Health Care, Many Do Without

Consider the case of a Des Moines family profiled by the Kaiser Family Foundation. Michael and Patty are the parents of two children. They make almost $36,000 per year, and both work in food processing plants. With two children at home, a mortgage, and many other bills, they have no money left over to purchase health insurance, even though Patty is eligible through her employer. If something happens to them or their children, they are forced to pay all their health care costs out-of-pocket.

Many believe that the United States has the best health care system in the world—the best treatments, the best medical technology, and the best pharmaceuticals. But this is like a cruel joke to the uninsured—including more than 8 million children—because they are forced to make do with substandard care or none at all.

Tom Harkin, "Access to Health Care: A Right, Not a Privilege," in www.harkin.senate
.gov, April 27, 2005.

The result is a paradox: The United States has a world-class health care system, but we fall behind most industrialized countries when our general health outcomes are measured. For example, members of minority groups are the least likely to have health insurance. Not surprisingly, they have higher rates of diabetes, heart disease, and HIV/AIDS.

One realistic solution would be to give everyone the option of joining the Federal Employees Health Benefits Program.

Health Care Should Also Cover Prevention

Bear in mind that health insurance is not just about seeing a doctor when you are sick. It's about prevention as well. If you have insurance you are more likely to have a relationship with a doctor who knows you and your health history. You are more likely to have access to preventive care so that chronic disease can be prevented in the first place. Without health care coverage, minor illnesses can turn into major ones. Small incidents can turn into chronic conditions. Once this happens, it becomes almost impossible to afford quality health insurance without restrictions on benefits.

Every American should have access to quality, affordable health care coverage. Why? Because people's lives, their livelihoods, and their ability to contribute to society are all undermined if they aren't healthy. In addition, access to health care coverage saves money in the long run. Overuse of emergency rooms, treatment of chronic conditions, and uncompensated care cost U.S. taxpayers billions each year.

Provide Citizens the Same Health Care that Government Workers Get

One realistic solution would be to give everyone the option of joining the Federal Employees Health Benefits Program. [The

Federal Employees Health Benefits Program covers federal employees, including members of Congress and their families.] Larger purchasing pools such as this are able to reduce insurance rates, guarantee coverage of existing conditions, and provide access to quality health care coverage. . . .

We have a simple message: In the world's richest nation, access to decent health care should not be a privilege restricted to some; it should be a right guaranteed to all.

No "Right" to Health Care Exists

Wayne Dunn

About the author: *Wayne Dunn is a contributor to the libertarian* Capitalism Magazine *and* The Objectivist. *He is also editor of the blog* The Rational View, *which advocates "reason, self-interest, individual rights and capitalism."*

A "right" to health care is the new opiate of the masses. And politicians are among the biggest pushers.

The Road to Health Care "Rights"

As with most druggies, America started off with the light stuff. It began in the sixties with the marijuana of socialized medicine, Medicare and Medicaid. We were at a (Democratic) Party and, hey man, other countries were doing it; so we inhaled. Now we're hooked.

Costly? We get by with a little help from our friends (taxpayers who foot the bill).

The habit worsened until the Clintons offered us the "right"-to-health-care bong. But Americans mustered the self-esteem to decline (thanks to a GOP [GOP stands for Grand Old Party, now known as the Republicans] intervention) and in 1994 checked into rehab by a Republican landslide.

But often junkies relapse. What America wouldn't stuff into the congressional crack pipe and smoke all at once, it's injecting into its political mainstream squirt by legislative squirt. Even the guys from the right-wing rehab center traded in their ties for tie-dyes and now support "rights" to prescription drugs.

Why "Right" Is Wrong

Why is a "right" to health care wrong? Why should we just say no? Because saying yes would not only achieve the opposite of the desired results, it would diminish real rights.

Legitimate rights don't place demands on other people. Your right to worship, for example, doesn't obligate me to take you to church or sing you a hymn. My right to free speech doesn't force you to toss me a megaphone or buy me some airtime. Your neighbor's right to pursue happiness doesn't require you to rent him a condo or fly him to Maui. Real rights demand only that you respect the rights of all. That's reality.

But then reality is what "right"-to-health-care addicts, like all druggies, are evading.

Health care is important, they say, people need it. But it's precisely because it's important, it's precisely because people need it that we must not blur the distinction between needs and rights. You may really need a romantic partner, for instance, but that doesn't mean you have a right to one. If you did, it would mean the forfeiture of that person's right to his or her own life, liberty and pursuit of happiness.

To the degree health care is made a "right," health care providers are enslaved.

Well, just as "rights" to other people's romantic favors would ravage their actual rights, so too would "rights" to other people's goods and services—which is what health care is. Phony rights demolish genuine rights.

Health Care Must Be Earned

Health care doesn't just pop into existence. It stems from individuals' intellectual achievements and productive abilities. It's the product of doctors and nurses spending a decade mastering their craft, of scientists toiling years to make life-saving breakthroughs, of capitalists staking fortunes on risky new ventures. And it's the product of businessmen transforming those dollars and breakthroughs into medicine and equipment, which doctors then bring to bear on human suffering.

Sure, we can pass a law giving you a "right" to all that. Heck, with enough votes, we can pass a law giving your house to the homeless (after all, they need it). But just because something's legal doesn't make it right. Slavery, remember, was legal.

And slavery is really what's at issue here: the enslavement of some to the needs of others. For to the degree health care is made a "right," health care providers are enslaved. Doctors, nurses, scientists and businessmen with too much self-respect to have their abilities declared your "right," will simply abandon medicine, leaving your medical future to those lacking such self-respect. (It's already begun.) Investment dollars will divert from health care interests into freer and thus more profitable areas. (That's begun, too.) Oh, but this has its upside: there'd be no gripes about the "high cost" of new prescription drugs—there'd never be any new drugs.

To preserve both health care and rights, Americans must quit health care "rights" cold turkey.

Bogus Rights

Walter E. Williams

About the author: *Walter E. Williams is a conservative and a professor of economics at George Mason University in Fairfax, Virginia.*

Do people have a right to medical treatment whether or not they can pay? What about a right to food or decent housing? Would a U.S. Supreme Court justice hold that these are rights just like those enumerated in our Bill of Rights? In order to have any hope of coherently answering these questions, we have to decide what is a right. The way our Constitution's framers used the term, a right is something that exists simultaneously among people and imposes no obligation on another. For example, the right to free speech, or freedom to travel, is something we all simultaneously possess. My right to free speech or freedom to travel imposes no obligation upon another except that of non-interference. In other words, my exercising my right to speech or travel requires absolutely nothing from you and in no way diminishes any of your rights.

Rights Do Not Include Involuntary Takings

Contrast that vision of a right to so-called rights to medical care, food or decent housing, independent of whether a person can pay. Those are not rights in the sense that free speech and freedom of travel are rights. If it is said that a person has rights to medical care, food and housing, and has no means of paying, how does he enjoy them? There's no Santa Claus or Tooth Fairy who provides them. You say, "The Congress provides for those rights." Not quite. Congress does not have any resources of its very own. The only way Congress can give one

American something is to first, through the use of intimidation, threats and coercion, take it from another American. So-called rights to medical care, food and decent housing impose an obligation on some other American who, through the tax code, must be denied his right to his earnings. In other words, when Congress gives one American a right to something he didn't earn, it takes away the right of another American to something he did earn.

We don't have a natural right to take the property of one person to give to another; therefore, we cannot legitimately delegate such authority to government.

If this bogus concept of rights were applied to free speech rights and freedom to travel, my free speech rights would impose financial obligations on others to provide me with an auditorium and microphone. My right to travel freely would require that the government take the earnings of others to provide me with airplane tickets and hotel accommodations.

The Role of Government Should Be Limited

Philosopher John Locke's vision of natural law guided the founders of our nation. Our Declaration of Independence expresses that vision, declaring, "We hold these Truths to be self-evident, that all Men are created equal, that they are endowed by their Creator with certain unalienable Rights, that among these are Life, Liberty, and the Pursuit of Happiness." Government is necessary, but the only rights we can delegate to government are the ones we possess. For example, we all have a natural right to defend ourselves against predators. Since we possess that right, we can delegate authority to government to defend us. By contrast, we don't have a natural right to take the property of one person to give to another; therefore, we cannot legitimately delegate such authority to government.

Three-fifths to two-thirds of the federal budget consists of taking property from one American and giving it to another. Were a private person to do the same thing, we'd call it theft. When government does it, we euphemistically call it income redistribution, but that's exactly what thieves do—redistribute income. Income redistribution not only betrays the founders' vision, it's a sin in the eyes of God. I'm guessing that when God gave Moses the Eighth Commandment, "Thou shalt not steal," I'm sure he didn't mean "thou shalt not steal unless there was a majority vote in Congress."

The real tragedy for our nation is that any politician who holds the values of liberty that our founders held would be soundly defeated in today's political arena.

Even Nations with Health Care Rights Are Moving Away from Universal Care

David Gratzer

About the author: *David Gratzer is a physician and senior fellow at the conservative Manhattan Institute.*

Government health-care enthusiasts in the United States have long looked to Canada as a leading light of health care fairness and equity. From a distance, Canada may seem to have it all: modern medicine and universal insurance. Up close, the story is quite different. In 2005, the Supreme Court of Canada called the system dangerous and deadly, striking down key laws and turning the country's vaunted health care system on its head. The ruling aptly symbolizes the declining enthusiasm for socialized medicine even in socialist nations. American legislators—such as those in the California Senate who approved a single-payer plan in 2005[1]—should take note.

The Supreme Court of Canada is arguably the most liberal high court in the Western world, having . . . endorsed the constitutionality of gay marriage and medical marijuana. Most legal scholars expressed surprise that the justices even agreed to hear this appeal of a health care case twice dismissed by lower courts. Involving a man who waited almost a year for a hip replacement, the bench decided that the province of Quebec has no right to restrict the freedom of a person to purchase health care or health insurance. In doing so, they struck down two Quebec laws, overturning a 30-year ban on private medi-

1. California did not end up with a single-payer statute.

cine in the province. The wording of the ruling, though, has implications beyond Quebec, and could be used to scrap other major parts of Canada's federal health care legislation.

Canada's Shift Toward Privatized Health Care

The decision isn't simply a surprise, it's an earthquake—as if a Soviet court had ruled that not only could a Russian entrepreneur open a chain of restaurants, but he could issue stock to finance the scheme.

What would drive the bench to such a profound ruling? Chief Justice Beverley McLachlin and Justice John Major wrote: "The evidence in this case shows that delays in the public health care system are widespread, and that, in some serious cases, patients die as a result of waiting lists for public health care."

This outcome would not have been possible without the persistence of one man: Jacques Chaoulli. A Montreal physician, Chaoulli was so angered when a government bureaucrat shut down his private family practice that he went on a hunger strike. After a month, he gave up and decided that only the courts could help his fight.

With an eye on a legal challenge, Chaoulli tried his hand at law school—but flunked out after a semester. Undeterred, he sought the help of various organizations to support his efforts. None would. He decided to proceed anyway, choosing to represent himself. His legal fight, costing more than a half million dollars, was funded largely by his Japanese father-in-law.

But Chaoulli was not completely alone. He asked one of his patients for help. A former chemical salesman with a bad hip, the patient agreed. Their argument was simple: Quebec's ban on private insurance caused unnecessary suffering since waiting lists have grown so long for basic care.

The Problems with Government-Funded Care

The woes of Chaoulli's patient are all too common. Canadians wait for practically any diagnostic test, surgical procedure, or specialist consultation. Many can't even arrange general care. In Norwood, Ontario, for example, one family doctor serves the entire town, and he can only take 50 new patients a year. The town holds an annual lottery to choose the lucky 50.

U.S. health care may have its woes, but the siren song of socialized medicine offers no solution.

According to Statistics Canada, approximately 1.2 million Canadians lack a family doctor and are looking for one. Others seek more urgent care. Toronto was shaken recently when the media reported that a retired hockey legend was forced to wait more than a month for life-saving chemotherapy because of a bed shortage at the largest cancer hospital in the country. American companies now routinely advertise in major Canadian dailies, offering timely health care—in the United States. No wonder that, a few years back, more than 80 percent of Canadians rated the system "in crisis."

And now the Supreme Court of Canada agrees. Moreover, it's not alone in tiring of the shortcomings of socialized medicine. Throughout Europe, the story is one of a slow but steady abandonment of public health care.

British prime minister Tony Blair recently won reelection on a platform that called for tripling the number of surgeries contracted out to private firms. Across the Channel, private medicine flourishes. Tim Evans of the influential think tank Centre for the New Europe observes: "There is no ideological debate about who provides the care [in continental Europe]. . . . There are only good hospitals and bad hospitals, not public and private ones." Even in Sweden, patients choose among public and private hospitals. St. Goran's, the largest hospital in Stockholm, is privately run and managed.

And yet, in the United States, legislators continue to flirt with socialized medicine. . . . These policymakers should realize that U.S. health care may have its woes, but the siren song of socialized medicine offers no solution. Indeed, even the Supreme Court of Canada recognizes that socialism for health care is a prescription for an early grave.

CHAPTER 2

Can the Existing American Healthcare System Be Saved?

Chapter Preface

L ike the seemingly irreconcilable differences between those who believe health care is a basic human right and those who believe it is a service to be sold on the free market, the question of whether America's existing health-care system can be saved sharply divides its critics—and *everyone*, it seems, is a critic.

Here's the paradox: both reformers and defenders of the existing system acknowledge that American medicine is more advanced, more cutting edge, than health care available elsewhere in the world. Take, for instance, the storied Mayo Clinic in Rochester, a small city of 89,000 in rural southeastern Minnesota—a health-care system so specialized and first-rate that it draws U.S. presidents as well as kings and prime ministers from all over the world to the care of its 1,500 physicians and scientists. Rochester's downtown streets are lined with the sort of luxury-goods shops otherwise found only in midtown Manhattan, Beverly Hills, and expensive resorts, thanks to the wealth brought by the clinic's powerful overseas patrons. Yet 78 miles north, in Minneapolis and Saint Paul, in the U.S. state that currently boasts the highest proportion of insured citizens, at least 30 percent of Twin Cities residents lack any health-care coverage.

Put another way, despite the technological wizardry of American medicine, its benefits remain poorly distributed: an increasingly larger share of U.S. citizens are uninsured and unable to afford even the most basic health care. American medicine may be one of this country's proudest boasts, but many of its services are unavailable to one-third of the population.

Conservative and libertarian critics view the health-care glass as half full: they emphasize the accomplishments of American medicine and look for market-driven solutions to extend the marvels of high-tech medicine to more U.S. citizens. They reject the claims of liberal critics that health-care costs have become so unacceptably high that they are bankrupting a significant minority of Americans. They favor approaches that are termed *market solutions*—that is, government deregulation and reliance on private businesses to lower costs and provide wider access.

Liberal and progressive critics see the health-care glass as half empty: they stress the unequal and declining coverage available to America's citizens and point to the present system's failure to close these gaps. They see the spiraling costs of managed care, the inefficiencies and inequities of the country's patchwork system of health-care provision, the increasing costs of malpractice insurance and malpractice court awards, and the rise in personal bankruptcies caused by medical expenses as evidence that the existing system can no longer hold. Rather than repair it, these critics say, the system must be fundamentally changed.

Reading the selections in this chapter, you are likely to be struck as much by the difference in tone between these opposing views as by their differing contents.

The Problem with the Health Care System Is Not Health Care But America's Tax Code

R. Glenn Hubbard

About the author: *R. Glenn Hubbard is dean of the Graduate School of Business and professor of Economics at Columbia University, a former chairman of the President's Council of Economic Advisors, and a visiting scholar at the American Enterprise Institute, a conservative think tank in Washington, D.C.*

Health-care demand and inflation are draining the resources of federal and state government agencies, employers, and the self-employed. Despite our national investment of $1.9 trillion, we get highly inefficient care—spectacular in certain respects, but rife with error, disorganized, and unaffordable or inaccessible to many. About 46 million Americans—one in six—go without health insurance. Six out of ten worry about going bankrupt because of a major illness. Is this the health care $1.9 trillion should buy?

Of course not—and no one thinks so. In 2005, together with John Cogan and Daniel Kessler of the Hoover Institution and Stanford University, I published a book, *Healthy, Wealthy, and Wise*, containing five basic policy proposals that would put consumers in charge of America's health-care system, save $60 billion a year, and provide health insurance to as many as 20 million people. These savings and increases in coverage occur through the power of removing impediments to private markets.

Health Care Problems Stem from Our Tax Code

We found that many of the problems in our health-care system stem not from what happens in the doctor's office or hospital, but what happens in our tax code. If, on the one hand, an employer pays for an employee's health coverage, it is a tax-free cost for both the company and the individual, therefore allowing for generous health-care coverage in large companies—especially those with union-negotiated contracts. If, on the other hand an individual must pay for the health-care costs out of pocket and these costs cannot be written-off, the medical expenses are more keenly felt and are, at times, hard to afford. This difference often results in the person avoiding to seek medical care until it is absolutely necessary—if at all.

Universal health insurance deductibility would drive health-care decisions down to the consumer level, creating efficiencies impossible in today's third-party-payer system.

Many policymakers are starting to see the problem. . . . The bipartisan *President's Advisory Panel on Federal Tax Reform* suggested capping the tax deductibility of health-insurance premiums so that employers could extend only so much coverage to their workers. And, if we could do so, removing all tax subsidies for health care would be the best answer. That outcome is most unlikely, and the key is to stop the tax bias against low-cost individually purchased health insurance. In our book, we propose making all health-care spending deductible. The difference in those policy suggestions is significant, but the effects would be similar. For once, all Americans would begin to manage the cost of their health care directly, instead of letting others worry about it.

Full Health-Care Cost Deductability Is Not a Giveaway

Some conservative critics seem to miss this point. They see in full deductibility of health-care costs a major giveaway to health consumers. Not at all. First, we already over-subsidize health care through tax deductibility—the problem is that the subsidization is highly uneven, and is available generally only for those who work for major employers. By creating a 100 percent, universal health deductibility at the consumer level, no matter where someone works or whether they work, our proposal would give everyone an incentive to demand total control over their health-care dollars, and take that control away from companies and unions.

If patients enjoyed the same deductibility for health-care spending as their employers, they would take greater control over their health-care dollars—and higher deductibles and co-payments would reduce overall health spending substantially. (Critics may want to check our empirical evidence on this point—or offer their own evidence to the contrary.) Right now, the insured patient rarely—if ever—sees the actual bill. Even heavy users of health-care services are rarely aware of the true cost of their desire for, say, brand-name drugs over generics. Instead of the vast giveaway some detractors foresee in our proposal, universal health [insurance] deductibility would drive health-care decisions down to the consumer level, creating efficiencies that are impossible in today's third-party-payer system.

Our proposal would reward discriminating consumers and, importantly, give people a way to profit financially from their own good health.

Create a Market for Health Savings Accounts

Full tax deductibility of health-care spending would accelerate the use of Health Savings Accounts (HSAs), which are probably the best thing to happen to health care in a generation.

Created by both President George W. Bush and the Republican-led Congress, these accounts allow individuals to create tax-free nest eggs to cover routine out-of-pocket medical costs. Were HSAs to be used more commonly, the same dynamic that determines how most people spend their money—trying to obtain the highest quality at the lowest price—would finally come to American health care. That would reward the best doctors and hospitals, and squeeze inefficiency out of the system.

Critics from the left sometimes say that HSAs put more of the onus of health costs on individuals. Tell that to the 46 million Americans who currently don't carry any insurance. By making such insurance for major medical events—such as emergency hospitalization and chronic illness—more affordable, HSAs and other consumer-driven health-care policy ideas broaden access to essential health care. That will help millions of Americans get the health care they currently can't afford.

The key is to promote the availability of low-cost insurance to individuals currently subject to costly state mandates.

A greater focus on consumer-driven health care requires further policy improvements: open and national health insurance markets, so that consumers have more choices in the kind of hospitals, doctors, and insurers they use; greater investments into health-information technology to identify and prevent errors before they occur; and reforms of medical-liability rules, so that good doctors and nurses can practice quality health care without being harassed by nuisance lawsuits.

Innovation Can Extend Coverage to All

Again, some conservative critics mistakenly think that federalization of our health-care insurance and regulatory markets would inherently be bad for health care. If one's default position is to fight national markets governed by national standards at all turns, I suppose there's no sense arguing the point. But let there be no doubt that national markets would work. . . . State-by-state health-insurance regulations . . . in effect create high insurance costs for captive consumers and benefits for some large insurers who alone can either lobby themselves out of trouble or maintain the product lines that each state requires. A few decades ago, banking was run this way, a situation remedied by national banking reform. Instead of the gargantuan national influence on banking that some feared, we have a true national market for a vital financial service—more choices, more products, and more usage. There are other ways to accomplish insurance-market reform, too, but the key is to promote the availability of low-cost insurance to individuals currently subject to costly state mandates.

These proposals are the kinds of ideas that deserve an airing. . . . Americans already expect innovation from their health-care system—new drugs, technology, research, and cures. Now, they should demand innovation in how we pay for all this quality medicine. Let's make sure we can deliver.

Eliminating Excessive Regulations Can Cure America's Health Care System

Scott W. Atlas

About the author: *Scott W. Atlas is a senior fellow at the conservative Hoover Institution at Stanford University and a professor of radiology and chief of neurology at Stanford University Medical School.*

In the debate over health-care reform in this country, it seems that one vitally important question is too often left out of the equation: Why should we expect the government to be responsible for providing medical care in the first place?

Government Controls Health Care Costs

Food, housing, and clothing are no less basic to our daily lives, and yet citizens don't want government bureaucrats to tell us what kind of cereal we can buy or how much it will cost. When it comes to health care, however, the assumption that government needs to be involved ignores the virtual stranglehold the government already exerts on health-care prices in this country and the failure of that system.

Despite the presence of private insurers in our health-care marketplace, it is the government that to a great extent controls the price of health care. It is bureaucrats who set the reimbursement rates that doctors and health-care providers use to set their pricing, rather than relying on the actual costs and profit margins for their services. The most overt example is in Medicare-covered health services, where bureaucrats set "rates of reimbursement." Some multiple of these Medicaredetermined rates also serves as the basis for a significant percentage of payments by private insurers. And *it is the federal control of the health-care dollar that has led to increased costs, delays in patient care, and frustrations for both doctors and patients.*

The real cure for rising health-care costs is ... eliminating the third-party-payer system that shelters patients from making cost-conscious decisions.

Christopher Conover of Duke University has estimated the cost of excessive regulation in the health-care market to exceed $339 billion, with a net cost of $169 billion—more than U.S. consumers spend every year on gasoline and oil. His figures show that the cost of the medical legal system alone, including litigation costs, court expenses, and defensive medicine, exceeds $80 billion.

Eliminate Government Regulation and Bring Costs Down

This artificial pricing structure that our government imposes on consumers and doctors is unique to health care, and it has done little to rein in costs or improve care. The real cure for rising health-care costs is direct payment from patient to doctor, eliminating the third-party-payer system that shelters patients from making cost-conscious decisions and results in massive administrative costs and the artificial pricing of medical care. Prices come down when the patient is the customer— not the government or other third-party payer. Patients consider cost when they spend their own money: refractive eye surgery, whole-body-screening CT [computerized tomography, a high-tech technique for creating three-dimensional images of body structures] scans, and other procedures have come down in price when market forces are allowed to operate without third-party interference.

The isolation of the consumer from paying for health care and the inordinate amount of control that government exerts over health-care costs represent a startling exception to the free market system that has served us so well in every other major service industry. This should lead us to ask the question, *on what basis does "government" become the solution for escalating health-care costs?* And why, when it has failed to rein in those costs in the past, should we expect even more government control to be the answer today?

Medical Bankruptcy Is an Overblown Threat; Most People with High Medical Bills Are Covered by Insurance

Gail Heriot

About the author: *Gail Heriot is a professor of law at the University of San Diego and a contributor to the conservative magazine* National Review.

"Half of Bankruptcy Due to Medical Bills—US Study." At least so said the Reuters headline in [the 2005] story. And similar stories in newspapers across the country agree. Soon it [would] be repeated as gospel on Capitol Hill and by the chattering classes everywhere. Understandably, middle-class Americans have started to feel a little queasy about their health and about the adequacy of their health insurance.

The fundamental problem is that it isn't true. Despite what the authors have encouraged us to believe, the Harvard study, entitled "*Illness and Injuries As Contributors to Bankruptcy,*" isn't really about medical bills, crushing or otherwise. It's about bankruptcies that can—at least if you're willing to stretch things a bit—be classified as medically related. It finds that 54.5 percent of all bankruptcies have "a medical cause." But "medical cause" is used as a term of art here. In fact, the study does not claim that injury or illness was the primary cause of those bankruptcies. And, perhaps more importantly, it does not claim that the bankruptcies were caused by the crush of medical bills.

Gail Heriot, "Misdiagnosed: A Medical-Bankruptcy Study Doesn't Live up to Its Billing," *National Review Online*, February 11, 2005. Copyright © 2005 by National Review, Inc., 215 Lexington Avenue, New York, NY 10016. Reproduced by permission.

Most Medical Expenses Do Not Bankrupt People

Don't get me wrong. Some bankruptcies are caused by crushing medical debt. But they aren't half of all bankruptcies, and the only way to create the impression they are is to jimmy the figures. For example, the study classifies "uncontrolled gambling," "drug addiction," "alcohol addiction," and the birth or adoption of a child as "a medical cause," regardless of whether medical bills are involved. Yes, there may be situations in which a researcher might legitimately want to classify those conditions as "medical," but a study that is being used to prove that Americans are going bankrupt as a result of crushing medical bills is not one of them. A father who has gambled away his family's mortgage payment is not likely the victim of crushing medical bills. Similarly, new parents who find they can no longer afford their previous lifestyle now that one of them has to stay home with the baby will usually find the obstetrician's bill the least of their problems. Babies are a financial hardship even when hospitals give them away free.

Nobody likes to pay $1,000 in medical expenses even when they get two years to do it in, but for most Americans . . . it is not catastrophic.

Maybe that's why only 28.3 percent of the surveyed debtors themselves agreed with the authors that their bankruptcy was substantially caused by "illness or injury." The rest put the blame elsewhere, even when the study labeled their problems as at least in part "medical."

Buried in the study is the fact that only 27 percent of the surveyed debtors had unreimbursed medical expenses exceeding $1,000 over the course of the two years prior to their bankruptcy. Presumably 73 percent—the vast majority—had medical expenses during that two-year period of $1,000 or less. Had that figure been recited up front, it would have been obvious that the proportion of bankruptcies driven by un-manageable medical debt was nowhere near half.

Nobody likes to pay $1,000 in medical expenses even when they get two years to do it in, but for most Americans (particularly those with enough at stake to seek the protection of bankruptcy) it is not catastrophic. Indeed, for many families it is utterly routine. Something else is going on in the overwhelming majority of these bankruptcies, whether it's gambling debt, drug or alcohol addiction, child care expenses, divorce, loss of a job, or just plain out-of-control spending. The authors' decision to include any case in which the debtor had paid out more than $1000 in medical expenses in the course of two years as a bankruptcy with a "medical cause" is not just questionable. It's downright misleading.

The authors [of the bankruptcy study] present the data in ways that encourage the reader to misidentify medical expenses as the leading cause of bankruptcy.

Tracking Big Debt Makes More Sense

What would be significant for the public to know is how common the cases of bankruptcy due to crushing medical debt actually are—debt in the range of $10,000 or more in a single year. That, however, is something the study is careful not to disclose, even though the raw data behind the study would appear to be sufficient to make such computations possible. Instead, at every turn, the authors present the data in ways that encourage the reader to misidentify medical expenses as the leading cause of bankruptcy.

For example, at one point the reader is told that the mean out-of-pocket medical expenditure for an illness-related bankruptcy is $11,854. But this is not the average for the 54.5 percent of bankruptcies that the study holds to have "a medical cause;" it's the average for the much smaller group (28.3

percent) in which the debtor agreed that illness and injury played a substantial role. And the $11,854 figure is not for the year or two prior to the bankruptcy, but for the entire period of the illness, which may be many years or even decades. Finally, and most importantly, it is a mean and not a median.* Just one truly catastrophic illness costing a total of $6 million over the course of any length of time would be enough to put the group's mean at above $12,000, even if nobody else in the sample ever spent a dime on medical bills. It's hard to see why a serious scholar would use the mean instead of the median if the point of the study is to demonstrate fairly that a large proportion of bankruptcies are caused by medical bills. Means don't show that.

A Political Agenda to the Study?

At least one of the authors—Dr. Steffie Woolhandler, a Cambridge Hospital internist and associate professor of medicine at Harvard, makes it clear that she does indeed have an agenda—health-care coverage that is universal and comprehensive. "Covering the uninsured isn't enough. We must also upgrade and guarantee continuous coverage for those who have insurance," she said in a statement. She went on to condemn employers and politicians who advocate what she called "stripped-down plans, so riddled, with co-payments, deductibles and exclusions that serious illness leads straight to bankruptcy."

But Dr. Woolhandler's diagnostic skills leave something to be desired here. If medical debt is not the problem in these bankruptcies, more comprehensive health-care coverage is not the solution. Indeed, in some cases, it may even be counterproductive. For employers (and employees), coverage without deductibles and co-payments will mean more expensive health-care coverage. Some may try to make up the difference by cutting corners on disability insurance or by hiring fewer employees. Will that in the long run lead to fewer bankruptcies? Or more? This study sheds no light on those questions. Only by torturing the data has Dr. Woolhandler made it appear that it does.*

---

*Mean is the average of all data; *median* is the datum that has half of all other data above it and half below it.

Our Existing Health Care System Has Failed to Contain Sky-Rocketing Health Care Costs

Paul B. Ginsburg and Cara S. Lesser

About the authors: *Paul B. Ginsburg is president of the Center for Studying Health System Change. He is the author of several RAND Corporation studies on health-care issues and holds a doctorate in economics. Cara S. Lesser is a health researcher at the Center for Studying Health System Change in Washington, D.C.*

In some respects, the more things change in health care, the more they stay the same. Managed care had its heyday and rapid decline. There were mergers and break-ups and an alphabet soup of new types of organizations, management strategies and payment arrangements.

To what end? In many respects, we're no better off than we were a decade ago. Roughly the same proportion of Americans—about 15 percent—lacks health insurance, and we've managed to hold steady only because public coverage has grown. Health care spending continues to absorb an ever-larger piece of America's overall economy, growing from 13.8 percent of gross domestic product in 1995 to 16 percent in 2004 to a projected 20 percent in 2005.

At the same time, disparities between health care "haves" and "have nots" have widened. And, although public consciousness has been raised about serious gaps in the quality of care, progress reducing medical errors and improving quality has been slow.

Paul B. Ginsburg and Cara S. Lesser, "A Decade of Tracking Health System Change," *Center for Studying Health System Change*, March 2006. Reproduced by permission. www.hschange.org

Increased Competition, Few Winners

Amid all the change, one thing is clear—competition for the health care dollar has become intense. Hospitals and physicians have moved to increase revenues. This may well be a legacy of managed care, which spurred hospitals and physicians to offer substantial price discounts to avoid losing patients to competitors. For physicians in particular, it is also a response to continued reimbursement pressures under Medicare and Medicaid.

The increasingly competitive health care system has spawned new challenges for policy makers, while problems related to access, cost and quality have endured.

There is more marketing and targeted capital investment in profitable service lines. Hospitals are advertising quality and convenience and offering programs that generally healthy people might not be aware they need. Rather than ignore longstanding differences in the relative profitability of services and depending on cross subsidies to offer a full line of services, hospitals have focused capital spending on more profitable services, most often cardiovascular, orthopedic and oncological care. Physicians are attempting to make up for stagnant fee levels for professional services by investing in facilities, such as specialty hospitals and outpatient surgical centers, and introducing more ancillary services, such as imaging, into their practices.

Since most of the increased competition is aimed at increasing service volume rather than improving quality and increasing efficiency, it's highly questionable whether these developments bode well for patients and those who pay the bills—primarily employers and government. Some of the increased competitive behavior might moderate the effects of hospital consolidation, with dominant hospitals now facing competition from physicians. But a downside to this type of competition is that it threatens hospital cross subsidies, which are depended upon to provide services for the uninsured and standby capacity, such as burn and trauma units, for communities. And, as physicians add the capacity to offer more services within their practices, the risk of self-referral conflicts has increased. Finally, marketing services to consumers who have an insurer to pay most of the bill is certain to raise costs for those who pay for insured care. To date, purchasers have not developed effective strategies to counteract the potentially costly results of intensified competition for profitable services.

Thus, the increasingly competitive health care system has spawned new challenges for policy makers, while problems related to access, cost and quality have endured. . . .

Backlash: The Growth of Consumer-Driven Health Care

The next health care backlash is already brewing, zeroing in on health care affordability. Just as the rapid expansion of managed care prompted consumers to move the health care system in a new direction, today's rapid growth of patient cost sharing likely will again engage the public—and this time the focus will be more directly on the need for cost control, something cited by President [George W.] Bush in his 2006 State of the Union address. Whether new consumer-driven health insurance products and greater price and quality transparency will empower consumers to rein in health care costs on their own remains to be seen. Regardless, it seems quite certain that the increased financial responsibilities and risks associated with these and more conventional insurance products will raise public awareness about health care costs and engender greater support at least for discussion of strategies to preserve affordability.

Threats to affordability are developing on two fronts. First, consumers are feeling the pinch directly as employers continue to pass more of the cost of health benefits to employees.

If health care costs continue to rise faster than workers' incomes, a growing number of employees will find themselves priced out of health insurance. And those with coverage will spend a greater proportion of their income on premium contributions and out-of-pocket costs, including deductibles and coinsurance.

Second, Americans are confronting the affordability problem as taxpayers. Rising health care costs are hitting public-sector programs with a double-whammy: Not only are current program commitments rising more rapidly than revenues, but demand for public coverage is increasing as rising health care costs push more people out of employer-based coverage. Visibility is greatest at the state level, where rapid growth in Medicaid spending is colliding with requirements to balance state budgets. Even if Americans were amenable to tax increases, keeping pace with the current trajectory of Medicaid growth would be a formidable challenge.

What we actually have is a collection of highly local health care systems . . . so fragmented that it is a misnomer to call them a "system."

On the Medicare front, the first wave of the 76 million baby boomers turns 65 in 2011, and financing of their care will begin shifting from the employment-based private insurance system to the publicly financed Medicare program. As a result, Medicare spending will accelerate sharply as more people join the program and as per capita spending growth remains unchecked. Financing the boomers' care will severely strain the federal budget, leaving fewer resources for competing spending needs and forcing policy makers to consider tough trade-offs, such as reducing benefits, raising taxes or allowing larger deficits.

In light of these trends, increased urgency to control costs seems inevitable. For now, purchasers are pinning their hopes on consumer-driven health care and increased patient cost sharing to help slow the rapid growth of health care costs. Whether successful or not, the increased financial responsibilities patients will face may pave the way for a more candid discussion about the inherent individual and societal trade-offs involved in keeping health care affordable. Recent history shows that public perception is a critical ingredient. How health care leaders and policy makers harness public awareness of the cost problem and shape public opinion about options to respond will greatly influence the direction of the health care system in the years ahead. But leaders thus far have been unwilling to acknowledge that there are no painless solutions, instead promising that popular initiatives, such as health information technology and quality reporting, will slow cost trends substantially.

Local Solutions for Local Problems

Because there are limits to how far people generally will travel for medical care, health care markets are—and likely will continue to be—local. We have repeatedly been struck by the differences in the configuration and dynamics of health systems across communities. In some communities, large multispecialty groups dominate physician practice, while in others they are non-existent. Academic medical centers are at the core in some markets, while other communities revolve around a collection of community hospitals. A single Blue Cross Blue Shield plan dominates some markets, while others have a number of competing national plans. Many of these differences are longstanding, rooted in historical developments specific to individual communities rather than recent mergers and market entries.

And, it is not just the collection of players that defines a community's health care system; there also are cultural differences in the public's tolerance for high numbers of uninsured, the degree to which major stakeholders attempt to work together to solve problems and the role of government regulation. Together, these attributes result in different environments and systems of care. Indeed, while we speak of the "American health system," what we actually have is a collection of highly local health care systems—many of which are so fragmented that it is a misnomer to call them a "system" at all.

Changes in health care delivery occur market by market, with notable differences in response to what are often common drivers. Consider how managed care developed in communities across the country. Markets with established integrated delivery systems and multispecialty physician groups moved more quickly into the experiment of global capitation, while communities without this infrastructure focused more on administrative controls on access to services.

The increased concentration of health plans at the national level has had remarkably little impact on the way they do business in local health care markets.

Today, there are differences in how competition for specialty services is unfolding across the country. In some places, the focus is on new specialty hospitals; in almost all markets, physicians are expanding the scope of services delivered in their offices. And the intensity of competition appears to be weaker in communities where prominent academic medical centers dominate the market and physicians are closely aligned with hospital systems.

Challenges to Change at Local Levels

The local nature of health care markets not only produces different results in different communities; it also influences how change occurs. Despite diversity in configuration, most local health care markets today are comprised of a concentrated set of players—a handful of hospitals and health plans and, in some specialties, a limited number of physician practices—

that must interact with each other repeatedly over time. While national and regional affiliations among plans and providers certainly help shape business strategies, recognition that success or failure is highly contingent on ongoing relationship with a small set of players is a strong force shaping health care organizations' behavior in local markets. Indeed, the increased concentration of health plans at the national level has had remarkably little impact on the way they do business in local health care markets.

The economic boom of the late-1990s shifted the balance of power in favor of providers.

Challenging the Local Status Quo

In some cases, the insularity of local health care markets can obstruct change, as organizations that are so interdependent can be reluctant to press one another too hard. Take for example the experience with tiered-hospital networks. In some markets, hospitals blocked health plan efforts to create tiers based on price and quality, by refusing to accept "non-preferred" status within a network. A number of local, employer-led initiatives to collect and disseminate information on hospital cost and quality of care met a similar fate, as key institutions simply refused to participate. Higher market concentration leads to higher prices, with recent literature showing that this applies to nonprofit hospitals as well. And a long-standing problem for hospitals is their dependence on referring physicians, which encourages accommodating—and sometimes costly—behavior. "Keeping the physicians happy" is the reasoning behind many hospital decisions to invest in expensive and duplicative technology, inefficient use of operating room time and slow adoption of information technology.

On the other hand, the interdependence of key organizations in communities' health systems can promote collaboration and produce positive results. For example, limited competition and mutual self-interest has prompted hospitals in some markets to work together to respond to emergency department crowding and related ambulance diversions. Similarly, relationships between large provider organizations and health plans in a community can facilitate agreement on uniform quality measures and reporting requirements, as has been the case with the pay-for-performance initiative in southern California.

National Forces, Local Changes

However, regional forces have sparked change in local markets. Take for example how health plans pressured hospitals and physicians in the early 1990s to cut costs and assume financial risk for patients' care. This phenomenon occurred across the country, albeit to varying degrees in different markets. What prompted health plans to suddenly act so aggressively in their local markets? Ultimately, the broader economic climate emboldened plans, as employers, many of whom compete in national or international markets, got serious about controlling costs during a severe recession, shifting employees into managed care products that had restrictive provider networks.

Employers Leave Employee's Insurance Behind

Likewise, just a few years later, the economic boom of the late-1990s shifted the balance of power in favor of providers, as employers became more concerned with recruiting and retaining employees than with controlling health care costs. The resulting sharp shift in power between providers and health plans in local health care markets across the country led to a spate of plan-provider contract showdowns, when many providers threatened and some actually dropped out of health plan provider networks as they sought better contract terms and payment rates. Again, it was a change in the broader economic climate and in how employers approached health benefits that prompted local organizations to act aggressively and challenge the status quo.

Physicians and Medicare Push for Change

Today, new physician ventures have become an important force driving change in local health care markets. Facing stagnant reimbursement rates for professional services, many physicians have turned to investments in specialty hospitals and outpatient surgery centers to supplement their income. These ventures have created new competition for traditional acute care hospitals and challenged longstanding relationships between hospitals and physicians.

Another driver of change is the new Medicare hospital quality initiative, which encourages hospitals to publicly report a small number of quality measures. While reporting is voluntary, hospitals must report to receive a higher inpatient payment rate update. In contrast to the numerous failed local efforts to spur quality improvement through public reporting, the Medicare initiative has been powerful enough to compel almost universal participation. And our 2005 site visits found that hospitals are focusing on improving performance on these measures to be ready for the possibility that patients, employers or plans might use the information to guide care decisions. Although it remains uncertain how extensively purchasers or consumers ultimately will use the data, providers today do not want to take a chance on an environment in which their local competitors are seen as having better quality of care. . . .

The Next Big Idea:
Consumer-Driven Health Care

One of today's most pervasive "next big ideas" is consumer-driven health care. The concept envisions empowered consumers armed with detailed cost and quality information and a significant financial stake in the cost of care playing an instrumental role in controlling costs and driving quality improvement. In the 12 local health care markets tracked intensively by HSC over the last decade, these critical ingredients of consumer-driven health care are not yet in place. And there is a danger that overselling this concept could cut short the time needed to refine it to make it more effective—much as what happened with managed care.

For example, many current products offer little effective information support for enrollees. There also has been little investment in refined benefit designs that would shield services such as accepted regimens for chronic disease management from high cost-sharing requirements, target higher cost sharing to services with limited benefit or uncertain effectiveness, and emphasize patient incentives to use higher-performing providers.

Pay-for-Performance

Another development that demonstrates the importance of getting the details right is the nascent pay-for-performance (P4P) movement. Whether P4P will turn into a passing fad or result in quality improvements and increased efficiency will rest largely on physician acceptance of the concept, which in turn will require thoughtful, manageable implementation of P4P initiatives.

We need to encourage our political and health care leaders to look beyond the next election . . . to . . . high health care costs, uneven quality and inequitable access.

Ultimately, a critical lesson from the rise and fall of managed care and the tidal wave of organizational change that accompanied it is that the devil is in the details to produce meaningful, enduring change in the organization and financing of the health care system.

Looking Back . . . Going Forward

Looking back, there has been tremendous change in the health system over the past decade, and while increasingly competitive, there has been little progress controlling costs or improving access and quality of care. Despite this discouraging finding, there are lessons to be learned from reflecting on the experiences of the past decade. Looking forward, it is clear that the public will need to be actively engaged in how the health system changes, and that policy makers and health care leaders will need to develop solutions that can win the hearts and minds of the American public if they are to have real traction over time.

At the same time, strategies to improve health care delivery need to acknowledge the local nature of health care markets and that this affects how change occurs and the extent of its impact. And finally, while much needs to be done to improve the health system and a sense of urgency will help inspire action, there needs to be recognition that meaningful change will not happen overnight.

We need to encourage our political and health care leaders to look beyond the next election or fiscal year and to talk more frankly about real solutions to the enduring problems of high health care costs, uneven quality and inequitable access.

America's Current System of Health Care Endangers Patients and Providers

Mehmet Oz

About the author: *Mehmet Oz is Professor of Surgery at Columbia University College of Physicians and Surgeons and a well-known transplant surgeon. He is coauthor of the bestseller* You: The Owner's Manual *(2005).*

His family trusted me with his care, but I knew little about my patient, except that he would die without a mechanical pump to support his failing heart. He had undergone unsuccessful emergency coronary bypass surgery elsewhere before being transferred to our hospital. In our possession were Xeroxed records from his old chart, which we used as part of our effort to piece together his medical history.

As we stood in the operating room ready to make the skin incision, a call from the insurance company was transferred in. The unconscious patient's policy covered heart transplantation but not the mechanical pump needed to keep him alive while awaiting a donor heart. Should I proceed with lifesaving surgery and potentially bankrupt our program, or should I hold off? In any case I could be sued, either by the patient's estate for denying care or by the insurance company for compelling them to spend several hundred thousand dollars to transplant the saved patient.

I write this editorial because I chose to operate, but unfortunately this is not always the case, even by esteemed healthcare providers. Ultimately we settled the insurer's complaint that if our team had not prolonged this man's life, the company could have avoided the transplant expense. More importantly, this gentleman has gone on to live a very productive life with his new heart.

A Healthcare System that Does Not Work

Nevertheless, the trust that this patient's family placed in medicine was not supported by America's health insurance system or our health information programs or our malpractice protection. He was protected by the deeply ingrained professionalism that permeates the culture of medicine, a tradition that is being eroded.

For example, our healthcare system offers inherently conflicting incentives arising from erratic insurance coverage rules. Many who read this piece may not be familiar with the subtleties of their own insurance policies. Ironically, 15 percent know their benefits precisely because they own absolutely no health insurance. As a result, other than emergencies, physicians and hospitals must factor in insurance concerns as the care of patients is discussed.

The locus of control in healthcare does not rest with anyone—not overwhelmed doctors, disenfranchised patients, or even those paying most of the bills.

Lack of a rudimentary national health information sharing system hinders accurate decision-making and quality control, especially as rudderless patients bounce around the healthcare system. Patients cannot negotiate their often-serpentine path to wellness without better road signs, and their doctors often do not have or make the time to serve as tour guides. Balkanized health information systems offer little continuity of care for patients and limited insights into whether the clinical care provided remains up to date. The resulting clinical errors cause an estimated 98,000 deaths annually.

Further, our medical malpractice adjudication procedures result in a form of "jackpot justice" that neither helps many of the harmed nor drives doctors and hospitals to improve the quality of care they provide. The costs to the system, including defensive medicine, are estimated at $50–100 billion a year.

A System Offering Little Accountability

In the end, the locus of control in healthcare does not rest with anyone—not overwhelmed doctors, disenfranchised patients, or even those paying most of the bills (businesses and government). This lack of accountability leads to proposed solutions that are only stopgap measures and do not address the root cause of the myriad concerns and complaints about our healthcare systems—a disintegration of trust.

Physicians appreciate this reality but they have lost their voice. Most Americans recognize that the medical profession has a rich heritage of placing the patient's interests first, continually improving proficiency, and regulating themselves. But doctors also have a civic duty to reveal the need for meaningful transformation of our nation's healthcare system. These sentiments are coalescing more as a movement than as an organization.

Together with the Columbia University's Institute for Medicine as a Profession, led by David Rothman, and the Center for Health Transformation, founded by Newt Gingrich [Republican and Speaker of the U.S. House of Representatives, 1995 to 1999], we have surveyed numerous physicians, nurses, health business leaders and laypeople using individual interviews and focus groups. Three broad themes have crystallized that could build trust in a 21st century intelligent healthcare system. What do the healthcare providers prescribe for America?

Physicians' Prescription for Health Care Reform

1. Modernized health information systems will reduce dangerous and expensive medical errors. Electronic patient records can be shared between doctors and brought together to produce meaningful outcomes data that support decision-making. Under such a system, both doctors and patients would be better informed and medical practice would be advanced. We need to build a national health information infrastructure that includes standards for collecting and sharing data to reduce wasteful paperwork and save money. Our banks should not have better information systems than our hospitals.

2. Progressive health justice programs should build trust by prompting doctors to more readily share the truth about unexpected outcomes with patients and colleagues. How else can we learn from the mistakes that humans taking care of humans are destined to make? Plus, the public benefits much more from solutions that reduce errors in care than from compensation systems for the few who win the litigation lottery. Many solutions have been offered, including creation of health courts (resembling tax courts) where expert panels could streamline payment of money to injured patients and families with less delay and overhead. Perhaps the few doctors who are dishonest with their patients about errors would be ineligible for these health courts.

3. Affordable health insurance for all is essential to protect the trust between doctor and patient and to avoid scenarios like the case described above. In addition, besides unnecessarily delaying their care, uninsured patients become expensive drains on our healthcare system, and we end up paying, anyway. A variety of plans have been suggested to achieve this goal, including subsidizing insurance premiums for the poor while compelling all

others to purchase a discounted minimum plan (as is the case with automobile insurance). We need to pick a program and get going.

These are not new ideas, but the power of doctors agreeing to push for change can be transformational. The public deserves honest insights from its healers, combined with earnest efforts from its elected officials, to act on these opinions. How else can we nurture the trust that saves lives? It kept my patient alive. Let's pass it on.

CHAPTER 3

Current
CONTROVERSIES

How Should Healthcare Be Reformed?

Chapter Preface

To a casual onlooker, post–World War II American health care appears to have gone through a number of fashions: first, in the 1950s–1960s, care provided by physicians in private practice, augmented by hospital-based clinics, laboratories, and other services; second, big federal and federal-state programs, Medicare and Medicaid, established by Congress in 1965 to provide care for disabled people and citizens over 65 (Medicare) and people who are impoverished (Medicaid); third, care provided by health maintenance organizations (HMOs), most popular in the 1970s–early 1990s; and most recently, care provided under high-deductible insurance policies purchased by people using health savings accounts (HSAs) and other consumer-driven health plans (CDHPs).

Each of these approaches has promised breakthroughs to Americans: private physicians, through their organization, the American Medical Association, proclaimed private medicine as the alternative to "creeping socialism" and the only system offering citizens true "choice"; Medicare and Medicaid brought federal and state governments into the role of health-care provision as an extension of New Deal and Great Society social programs; HMOs touted themselves as the only system emphasizing prevention, wellness, and cost containment. Most recently, HSAs have been promoted by the Bush administration and other supporters as the only system that brings down costs and awards individual responsibility.

If there's a fair amount of skepticism among Americans about our present health-care system, it is partly because of the failure of these systems to deliver on some of their promises.

Conservative and libertarian policy makers, politicians, and care providers are most attracted to limited system fixes: consumer-driven health care plans, particularly HSAs; nationwide competition among existing health plans; deregulation; and tax and tort reform. By encouraging HSAs, these reformers hope to encourage personal savings, lower private insurance-policy costs, and reward healthy behavior among policy holders. By opening existing health-care systems to nationwide competition, some of them believe that the economies of scale made possible by larger systems can bring down health-insurance costs. By eliminating state mandates on the coverage that health insurers must provide to individuals—for example, mammograms, tests for diabetes and colon cancer, and childhood immunizations—some of them hope to lower the average cost of health-care coverage. By whittling down federal regulations governing hospital, clinic, and other health-care institutions, some of them believe the administrative costs associated with recording and reporting to the federal government would decline. By changing the tax code so that individuals could deduct the full cost of their private health-care plans and by limiting awards in court cases involving medical malpractice, some of these reformers hope to improve the existing system without altering its essentially private nature.

Liberal and progressive reformers reject consumer-driven health plans as solutions to America's health-care crisis. They point to the failure of managed care—once heralded as the solution to America's health care woes—to lower costs and extend coverage to uninsured individuals. They deplore the inconsistency of an industry divided into many self-contained systems that increase administrative costs through duplication and excessive gatekeeping [see glossary] and that impede providers' communications within and between competing systems. They view the emergence of HSAs as plan-of-choice among conservatives as little more than tax giveaway to wealthy individuals at the expense of plans that could extend coverage to more Americans. To these critics, nothing short of a radical restructuring of American health care toward universal, government-provided coverage and away from market values and practices can solve the present crisis.

You might well be wondering if factions with two such opposing visions can even talk to each other, and you would be right: to date, dialogues between partisans of these fundamentally opposed positions have generated much more heat than light, as this chapter illustrates.

Consumer-Driven Health Care Prompts People to Spend Less on Health Care

Devon M. Herrick

About the author: *Devon M. Herrick, Ph.D., is a senior fellow at the conservative National Center for Policy Analysis in Dallas, Texas. His research interests include Internet-based medicine, health insurance and people who are uninsured, and pharmaceutical drugs.*

Consumer driven health care is a new paradigm for health care delivery. Defined narrowly, consumer driven health care refers to health plans in which individuals have a personal health account, such as a health savings account (HSA) or a health reimbursement arrangement (HRA), from which they pay medical expenses directly. The phrase is sometimes used more broadly to refer to defined contribution health plans, which allow employees to choose among various plans, often with a fixed dollar contribution from an employer. Those who opt for plans with rich benefits may have to contribute a significant amount of their own money in addition to an employer's contribution. Those with more basic coverage contribute less of their own money.

How Consumer-Driven Health Care Is Different

More choice and greater control over one's health plan are characteristics of a consumer-driven health care market place. People with personal health accounts have economic incentives to better manage their own care. The reason: In addition to health benefits, they realize economic rewards for making good decisions and bear economic penalties for making bad ones. These economic incentives make patients more likely to seek information about medical conditions and treatment options, including information about prices and quality. Patients will respond to these incentives in different ways. Some will seek information about diseases, treatments and health care providers over the Internet, including comparative information about treatment outcomes of individual health care providers and the fees they charge. Some may bypass primary care physicians and directly order their own diagnostic tests or seek online consultations. Others may bypass brand name drugs and obtain less expensive genetic substitutes, therapeutic substitutes and over-the-counter drugs. In general, people will consume fewer medical services, and pay less for health care in the long run when they are spending their own money. . . .

According to a recent survey of patients visiting an internal medicine practice, . . . 54 percent had used the Internet to gather health information.

Whether they like it or not, patients are likely to manage more of their own care in the future. This is the result of several trends.

Patients Can Access More Medical Information

With the advent of the Internet and the case of access to medical information, patients no longer have to rely on physicians to answer every question. They can obtain medical information directly. The growth of the Internet and the vast amount of information it makes available are leading to dramatic changes in information delivery. About 80 percent of adult Internet users (estimated at 93 million people) have searched for health information online. Estimates vary, but by most accounts there are approximately 20,000 health-related Web sites. These activities constitute a sharp break with the tradition of doctors as the sole source of health related information. In the past, much of the medical literature was available only at large libraries, medical schools or by subscription to expensive scholarly medical journals. Now, much of this literature is readily available to anyone with Internet access.

According to a recent survey of patients visiting an internal medicine practice, more than half (54 percent) had used the Internet to gather health information. Of these, about, six-in-ten (59 percent) rated the information "the same as" or "better than" information they got from their doctors. An equal number (60 percent) did not discuss the findings with their physician.

More than two-thirds of the public (72 percent) thinks "insufficient time spent by doctors with patients" is one cause of preventable medical errors.

Another way patients find out about medicine is *direct-to-consumer* advertising, which is mostly about drug therapies. Drug advertising benefits patients because it educates them about new treatments and often prompts them to seek care for previously untreated medical problems. In 2000, drug manufacturers spent $2.5 billion on direct-to-consumer advertising; about $1.5 billion dollars was spent to promote a mere 20 drugs.

More Treatment Options Are Available

Medical science has made enormous advances in the past few decades, increasing the range of therapies available to patients. Prescription drug therapy is an area where consumers have the most choices. For example, U.S. companies developed 370 new medicines within the last decade alone, according to the Pharmaceutical Research and Manufacturers of America. . . .

Doctors Can't Manage Patients' Care

In the past, many patients had a "personal" physician who met most of their health needs. In addition to examinations and treatments, doctors also were responsible for patient education. The ongoing relationship between the physician and patient was an information exchange, in which patients told their doctors about their symptoms and doctors provided diagnoses and recommended treatments. This trusting relationship has changed for a number of reasons. Among them: 1) Increasing medical specialization means that no single physician can provide all the information patients need, and 2) Physicians do not have enough time to give their patients complete information on their health. As medical knowledge has grown, an increasing proportion of doctors have specialized so that no individual physician can provide all the care a patient may need. Even within their specialties, doctors have trouble staying current in their field. About 10,000 clinical studies occur every year, and by some accounts, medical knowledge doubles every 42 months. . . .

A Harris Poll found that even when physicians offer to answer patients' questions, 60 percent of patients forget some of the questions they mean to ask. Moreover, patients retain only a fraction of the information they receive from their physician during an office visit. People think this lack of communication affects the quality of patient care. For instance, more than two-thirds of the public (72 percent) thinks "insufficient time spent by doctors with patients" is one cause of preventable medical errors, and three-fourths (78 percent) think that the occurrence of medical errors could be reduced if physicians spent more time with patients.

Physicians will always serve an important role advising patients about their medical needs. But patients need other options. Patients seeking medical information on their own are partially substituting for the service of physicians. A few hours spent on the Internet may substitute for a costly face-to-face office visit.

Managed Care Created Distrust of Insurers

In the 1980s and 1990s, employers began replacing fee-for-service health plans with managed care in an attempt to reduce their health care costs. Managed care organizations tried to hold costs down by negotiating deeply discounted fees with providers and by limiting access to services they deemed unnecessary. They often limited doctor discretion and replaced it with protocols for managing patient care. In many cases physicians were directly employed by health insurers and given financial incentives to withhold or limit access to types of care the insurance companies considered wasteful or costly. Even today, nearly one-third (31 percent) of U.S. physicians report they sometimes do not discuss useful treatments that are not covered by insurers.

Americans have a powerful new tool with which to educate themselves and manage their own health care needs: the World Wide Web.

Practices like these led to a consumer backlash in the 1990s, as patients saw managed care as a threat to their health and well-being.

Employers Are Requiring Workers to Share More Costs

Employers are increasingly shifting health care costs and risks to employees. For instance, during the period from 1993 to 2004, the average annual deductible workers with conventional health plans had to pay before insurance began to pay rose an average of 86 percent from $222 to $414. For family plans, the deductibles rose by 74 percent ($495 to $861). Over the past 10 years Preferred Provider Organizations (PPOs) [group health-care systems organized by insurance companies using doctors, hospitals, clinics, and other providers who work on contract to the insurer] with higher deductibles have been replacing first-dollar HMO plans. PPO coverage has risen from 27 percent of all covered employees to 58 percent. PPO plans have higher deductibles and 31 percent of PPOs used by small employers now feature in-network deductibles of $1,000 or more.

More employers are offering consumer-driven health plans, which usually include high deductible health insurance coupled with personal health accounts which workers use to pay for their incidental medical spending. A recent Milliman employer survey found that almost all (98 percent) employers are considering offering high deductible health plans, whereas in 2003 less than half (48 percent) considered offering them. In 2002, only about one percent of workers (1.5 million people) had health plans featuring personal health accounts. According to a new estimate by Forrester Research, the number of people with health savings accounts could grow to 18 million, with $35 billion in assets, by 2012.

How Patients Are Managing Their Care

Americans have a powerful new tool with which to educate themselves and manage their own health care needs: the World Wide Web. The Internet is a portal to medical libraries and Web sites with disease-specific information, and it gives patients direct access to prescription drugs, direct laboratory testing services, and therapeutic alternatives.

Obtaining Information on Conditions and Treatments

The Internet allows access to medical information that was unavailable to ordinary Americans only a decade ago. And people are responding. In 1997 the National Library of Medicine eliminated fees to search its "MedlinePlus" Web site, the world's largest medical library, and the number of searches rose from about seven million a year to 180 million—about 60 million of which were by the general public rather than medical professionals. The American College of Physicians Foundation encourages doctors to send patients to Medline-Plus, a practice referred to as writing prescriptions for "information therapy." . . .

Two-thirds of people who seek health information on the Internet search for information on specific diseases. . . .

- Most people (83 percent) search for medical studies.

- Seventy-one percent go to the Web sites of medical societies.

- About 39 percent go to the Web site of nonprofit organizations, such as patient advocacy organizations and disease research groups.

- Thirty-eight percent search Web sites for information about clinical trials for new therapies.

- Almost one-third (32 percent) go to commercial health Web sites, such as product-specific sites maintained by drug companies.

Obtaining Advice from Physicians

Most patients with Internet access (90 percent) would like the ability to consult their physician by e-mail, according to a Harris Interactive poll. However, only a few doctors offer patients the ability to request services or prescriptions by e-mail. According to a 2001 survey, only about 14 percent of patients exchange e-mail with their physicians and only a tenth of these do so on a frequent basis.

One obstacle to e-mail consultations is that few insurance companies will reimburse physicians for this service. Some health plans will not compensate doctors for e-mail exchanges unless the patient has first been examined in an office. Other insurers reimburse less for e-mail exchanges than for in-person visits. However, this is changing. For example, Blue Shield of California pays physicians the same for an e-mail consultation ($25) as it does for an office visit. Furthermore, in January 2004, the American Medical Association created a reimbursement code for online consultation patients, making it easier for physicians to get paid.

Do-it-yourself tests are proliferating, making self-diagnosis easier than ever before.

Physicians who exchange e-mail with their patients find it often replaces telephone consultations. But patients who send e-mail messages tend to spend more time composing their thoughts and create more focused messages than they do for phone conversations. An example of this new paradigm is Alan Dappen, M.D., who practices medicine almost entirely by telephone and e-mail contact. His time is billed in 5-minute increments and ranges from $25 for in-office visits to $15 phone consultations with patients who have set up prepaid accounts.

Obtaining Diagnoses Without Costly Visits

Patients have access to an increasing number of medical tests to assess the state of their health and diagnose their ailments. They can now order a variety of tests directly that were once exclusively available only at a physician's request. But they often have to pay for these tests [out] of pocket. Many tests are offered by pharmacies and other retailers over the counter. Sales of self-diagnostic over-the-counter tests tripled from $750 million in 1992 to $2.8 billion in 2002.

Home pregnancy-testing kits have been available for years. In fact, they have become so ubiquitous that they are sold in grocery stores everywhere. In some cases, they can be purchased at inexpensive "dollar stores" for $1 a piece. High quality pregnancy test strips are available in bulk on eBay.com for 50 cents apiece. Pregnancy tests were followed on to retail store shelves by ovulation predictor tests.

Do-it-yourself tests are proliferating, making self-diagnosis easier than ever before. These include tests for HIV, prothrombin time (clotting) for bleeding disorders and hepatitis C infections. For example, ear infections are the number one reason children see a doctor—accounting for 20 million office visits annually. The EarCheck Middle Ear Monitor is a home testing device for inner ear infections that uses sonar to check behind the eardrum for fluids that may indicate ear infection. The monitor costs about $50, an amount roughly equal to the fee for a single office visit. . . .

Numerous tests can now be done on blood, and many of these are readily available to patients without a doctor's prescription. Another option that may soon be available to patients is screening storefronts or kiosks that offer lab tests in a convenient setting and provide results quickly, without consulting a physician. . . .

One firm, Quest Diagnostics, has aggressively moved into the field of patient-ordered medical testing. The Web site QuesTest.com features a health library that patients can use to learn more about the tests Quest offers. Another medical testing laboratory, HS Labs (BloodWorksUSA.com), allows patients to pay a fee online, then stop by one of a nationwide network of collection points where a lab technician can draw a blood sample. . . .

Patients can also order genetic tests to determine their risk for cancer or heart disease and diagnostic imaging to discover if disease is present. Prices for patient-ordered genetic testing for susceptibility to breast and ovarian cancer range from $586 for a single point mutation to $3,312 for a complete sequence. Patients can also order "virtual exams" using MRI or PET technologies to detect cancer, heart disease and other conditions. Many physician groups oppose the use of patient-ordered body scans in asymptomatic patients because these often yield ambiguous results that require patients to spend money on follow-up tests. However, medical societies support doctor-ordered preventive screening tests for various conditions at ages called for in medical protocols. Patients who are aware of the recommended screenings can order many of those tests themselves, for less than a doctor would charge. The difference: Patients typically have to pay for scans they seek out themselves out of pocket, whereas doctor-ordered tests are more likely to be reimbursed by insurers.

Self-Treatment Is Lowering Patients' Costs

According to an article in the *British Medical Journal*, only one out of every 40 symptoms results in a patient making an office visit for a medical consultation. For example, it has been estimated that, at some point in their lives, between 15 percent and 40 percent of the general population experiences gastrointestinal symptoms such as rectal bleeding, irritable bowel syndrome, and dyspepsia (chronic indigestion). Yet only a quarter to a third of people experiencing these symptoms ever consults a practitioner. The information they obtain on the Internet often allows patients to make their own decisions about which symptoms require consultations.

For most medical conditions, people initially self diagnose and treat symptoms, usually with over the counter (OTC) drug remedies. OTC drug products account for 60 percent of drugs used by Americans. Estimates vary, but according to Rottenberg, Americans buy OTC drugs about 12 billion times a year. . . .

Eighty-nine prescription drugs, including specific-strength doses of some drugs, have been switched to over-the-counter since 1975. Millions of Americans use these drugs. For example, first generation antihistamines are a popular class of drugs sold over the counter with 14 different formulations available since 1975. It is estimated that 20 million allergy sufferers were self-treating with OTC (sedating) antihistamines in 2002, almost half of the total number of Americans suffering from allergies. . . .

Patients Can Comparison-Shop for Drugs

Consumers have never had more opportunities to obtain price information about drugs. A patient with a prescription can find a range of prices by clicking on a few Internet pharmacy Web sites. The Internet makes it easy to look up information on government and private programs to assist elderly, low-income and disabled patients. Additionally, Web-based services help patients find comparable medications that are cheaper than their current prescriptions. Patients can cut costs substantially by becoming aggressive consumers. In fact, seniors can reduce the cost of some common drug therapies by more than 90 percent if they use the same buying techniques they routinely use when shopping for other goods and services. . . .

Self-Monitoring and Treatment of Chronic Conditions

Treatment of chronic diseases is one of the factors driving up health care costs. Nearly half (45 percent) of all Americans have a chronic condition, and half of those (60 million) have multiple chronic conditions. A Yale University study found that one-quarter of Americans have one or more of five chronic conditions: mood disorders, diabetes, heart disease, high blood pressure and asthma. Moreover, patients with these conditions account for almost half of all health care spending.

Patients with chronic illnesses can use the Internet to obtain information on specific medical conditions, clinical trials and the latest drugs. They can also share their experiences with and learn from others suffering from the same conditions. Once patients inform themselves, they can manage their conditions and control their health care in ways unheard of only a few decades ago. . . .

Legal Obstacles to Self-Care

State and federal regulation of medical care has not kept up with the technology now available to patients. Neither has it kept up with patients' ability to easily participate in their own medical decisions.

It would cut costs if a patient receiving comprehensive blood tests through a direct testing facility could choose a physician anywhere in the country (or world) to interpret the results.

Reform Is Needed on Laws on Physician Practice

In the United States, physicians are licensed by a state medical board to practice medicine. Many state medical boards find the practice of cyber-medicine unethical if a consultation does not involve face-to-face examinations. This makes practicing medicine online and across state borders difficult—if not illegal. Even rendering second opinions by way of the Internet is sometimes problematic. For example, physicians working for the Web-based service MyDoc.com faced the threat of legal action for treating patients after having online consultations. However, 43 percent of Internet-using patients report seeking, in effect, a second opinion on a medical Web site. About one-third of patients on the Internet have sought the advice online of a physician other than their own.

State medical licensing also restricts trade. A patient receiving a mammogram or body scan could request that the results be sent electronically to a high-tech facility in India to be interpreted by a highly trained Indian physician at a fraction of the cost of an American radiologist. Likewise, it would cut costs if a patient receiving comprehensive blood tests through a direct testing facility could choose a physician anywhere in the country (or world) to interpret the results. A few hospitals have arrangements with high-tech facilities staffed with Indian radiologists who interpret X-rays and scans at night when an American radiologist is not available. However, various state laws make this arrangement difficult unless the Indian radiologist is licensed in the state where the hospital is located or unless a state-licensed American physician signs off on the results.

Reform Is Needed on Laws on Referrals

Regulation also affects how medical referrals are made. State and federal laws prevent practitioners from paying fees in return for patient referrals. Although this sounds like a good policy, it also has some negative ramifications. Blocking all referral fees makes it difficult to connect patients with providers of medical services.

Imagine a medical services auction Web site similar to eBay. Sellers could offer package deals for various medical services available at given time slots. Potential buyers could read feedback left by previous patients to ensure the service provider's quality and honesty. Shady practitioners would be essentially blacklisted by accumulated negative feedback and no one would be willing to patronize them. But, because they are not able to charge physicians a referral fee, medical auction Web sites have to trust consumers to pay for completed services (although the patients have little incentive to do so after they have connected with a physician). And consumers are often difficult to track down since they likely only purchase services occasionally. Neglecting to report the purchase of the service to the Web site could save them $20 to $95 depending upon the procedure purchased. For this reason, most Web sites advertising medical services are promoting the services of individual medical practices rather than bringing together numerous physicians to compete on price to earn patients' business. As a result, the online market for connecting buyers and sellers of medical services is small and uncompetitive compared to the numerous auction Web sites like eBay and Yahoo.

One medical auction Web site that does exist, BidForSurgery .com, connects cosmetic surgery providers with potential patients. Physicians compete for business on both quality and price. . . .

Reform Is Needed in Regulation of Drugs

Two-thirds of office visits to physicians result in prescription drug therapy because it is among the most efficient methods to treat illnesses. But only a licensed medical practitioner can prescribe prescription drugs. . . . The process of moving a drug from prescription-only status to OTC status is called Rx-to-OTC switching. Drug manufacturers usually request this switch when their patent protection is about to expire. In other words, OTC drugs are usually older therapies that have been replaced by a newer medicine. In many cases newer drugs are more effective than older, less expensive drugs.

A different malpractice standard for e-mail consultations . . . is needed so that physicians are not afraid to use e-mail with patients.

Restricting patent medications to the· prescription-only market drives up consumers' costs. Likewise, denying consumers access to any safe drug drives up treatment costs. The Food and Drug Administration (FDA) has recently shown a greater willingness to consider increasing patients' access to formerly prescription-only drugs. Consequently, the number of drugs switched to OTC status is expected to increase 50 percent over the next few years. . . .

Reform Is Needed on Legal Liability

Physicians usually counsel patients on treatments and therapies in person and then write relevant information in the medical records based on the physicians' observations. Whereas there is usually no complete documentation of phone conversations or examination room visits, an e-mail exchange is often an unfiltered transcript of patient and physician exchanges. Physicians may risk lawsuits if an e-mail exchange in the medical record is not concise in its explanation of patient treatment plans and does not conform to standards of accepted care protocols. A bigger problem is that there is no examination on which advice is given. The American Medical Association recommends that physicians establish guidelines for situations when e-mail correspondence is appropriate and when in-person office visits are preferred. A different malpractice standard for e-mail consultations (compared to in-person consultations) is needed so that physicians are not afraid to use e-mail with patients out of fear of malpractice suits. . . .

Consumers now have numerous avenues to become smart shoppers of medical services. Research has shown that employees are more satisfied when they have a greater choice of plans and consumer-driven health care offers them the ultimate choice. With these new plans comes the opportunity to manage our own care.

High-Deductible Health Plans Bring Down Insurance Costs for Consumers

Scott W. Atlas

About the author*: Scott W. Atlas is a senior fellow at the conservative Hoover Institution at Stanford University and a professor of radiology and chief of neurology at Stanford University Medical School.*

Health care was a top domestic issue in [2004's] presidential campaign. No wonder. No one is happy with the current system. Patients and doctors view it as bloated, unnecessarily complex, restrictive, and increasingly costly. Employers view rising costs as a major deterrent to expanding their job pool. The question is how to best remedy the problem. There [were] two competing approaches advanced in the presidential debate. Only one, I believe, represents a cure.

Rising Costs Are the Result of Patients Not Knowing Costs of Care

There has been a serious misdiagnosis of the problem of rising costs. Advanced medical technologies are often blamed, but that is not correct. The main problem is our third-party payer system. The absence of direct payment from patient to doctor for most medical expenses has shielded Americans from considerations of cost. It creates the illusion that "someone else is paying" and fosters the idea that patients are entitled to all medical care, regardless of cost. That is a costly illusion. It is also the heart of our problem.

Consideration of price is an essential component of a free market economy, and health care is no exception. Third parties now pay an unprecedented 85 percent of health-care costs. This encourages patients to neglect cost and overspend.

How did the major party candidates say they [would] fix the problem?

Senator John Kerry wanted to shift more costs to taxpayers, which would in fact expand third-party coverage. His plan [would have] added $895 billion to the cost of the system over 10 years, according to the Commonwealth Fund.

High-Deductible Plans Lower Costs

The Bush administration's Medicare Act of 2003 offered a much different approach. It offered high-deductible health plans to cover unanticipated and significant expenditures but not the vast array of routine expenditures now covered by most health plans. This makes enormous sense. After all, we do not expect our homeowner's insurance to reimburse us when light bulbs need replacing or when the kitchen sink gets clogged or when the gutters need to be cleaned.

High deductibles ... eliminate small claims and thereby reduce administrative costs, projected to exceed $200 billion yearly by 2012 ... rising faster than any other health-care cost.

Under this change, patients [would] pay directly for most medical expenses. This shifts power to the patient, not cost. Incentives for value-consciousness thus enter the decision process. That alone should significantly reduce expenditures.

Raising deductibles also makes health insurance more affordable. The high cost of coverage is the major cause of the rising number of uninsured, as many employers have withdrawn health insurance from benefits packages. Health services researchers Jason Lee [Academy for Health Services Research and Health Policy] and and Laura Tollen [Kaiser Permanente Institute for Health Policy] report that a combination of 30 percent coinsurance with a $1,000 deductible would reduce premiums 44 percent. According to their study, savings in health insurance premiums would approach 50 percent by raising deductibles to $2,000.

High deductibles . . . eliminate small claims and thereby reduce administrative costs, projected to exceed $200 billion yearly by 2012 and rising faster than any other health-care cost, aside from prescription drugs.

I understand concerns about people adjusting to a system in which they pay for previously covered care. First, the Medicare Act of 2003 established tax-favored Health Savings Accounts, or HSAs, which allow us to deposit money targeted for health care up to $2,600 for individuals or $5,250 for families.

Self-Directed Health Care Belongs to the Consumer

These accounts are a vast improvement over previous health-care savings plans. Higher caps on contributions are allowed, so high deductibles can be covered, and HSAs are allowed to accumulate, tax-free, without being subject to "use it or lose it" rules. Also, these accounts are owned by the individual rather than the employer and are fully portable. Deposits to the accounts would come from cost savings of lower premiums for the new high-deductible plan.

These accounts are right in step with our shift toward self-directed health care. According to a recent study, the percentage of consumers who unquestioningly follow their doctors' recommendations fell from 53 percent in 2000 to 36 percent in 2002. Moreover, physicians—at 27 percent—rank as the second-most important source of information for patients, far behind the Internet, with 37 percent of consumers using the latter to research hospitals, physicians, medical conditions, and insurance plans.

Can consumers make appropriate decisions about health care? The answer is a resounding yes. Arguments against empowering the patient for health-care decisions beg comparisons to the automobile industry and to self-directed retirement accounts, industries where consumer decision making is the status quo.

The next president simply needs to trust the people with their own money. That is the cure, plain and simple.

Thorough Privatization Will Provide Needed Reforms

John C. Goodman

About the author: *John C. Goodman, Ph.D., is the founder and CEO of the National Center for Policy Analysis (NCPA), a conservative think tank in Dallas, Texas. He is a theorist and strong proponent of Health Savings Accounts and author of nine books. The NCPA's Web site credits him "with playing a pivotal role in the defeat of the Clinton administration's plan to overhaul the U.S. health care system."*

In his [2006] State of the Union address, President [George W.] Bush devoted only a few sentences to health policy. But as the president was speaking, the administration released a five-page document describing health policy proposals so sweeping and bold, they are comparable in scope to Hillary Clinton's proposals of a decade ago. If the White House devotes the energy and political capital necessary to see them through, these reforms will leave a lasting mark on social policy in this country.

In 2003, the president signed legislation that theoretically allows every nonelderly American to establish a Health Savings Account (HSA). His proposed [2006] changes [would] make HSAs more affordable, flexible and available to more people.

HSAs Empower Individuals

The idea behind HSAs is quite simple. Individuals should be able to manage some of their own health care dollars through accounts they own and control. They should be able to use these funds to pay for out-of-network doctors, diagnostic tests

John C. Goodman, "Bush's Answer to Hillarycare," *NCPA Brief Analysis*, March 14, 2006. Copyright © 2006 National Center for Policy Analysis. All rights reserved. Reproduced by permission.

and other out-of-pocket expenses. They should be able to profit from being wise consumers of medical care and by having account balances that grow tax-free and eventually become available for nonmedical purchases.

To enable people to make more of these types of decisions on their own, the president [proposed] to (1) increase the amount people can contribute to their HSAs, (2) make it easier for people to obtain one and (3) encourage everyone to have one. (The tax breaks, portability and chronic illness features described below apply *only* to HSA plans.)

The main reason companies today provide their workers with health insurance rather than pay higher wages is the tax law.

Patients ... respond to the financial incentives created by HSAs in different ways. Some ... seek information about diseases, treatments and health care providers over the Internet. Some ... bypass primary care physicians altogether and directly order their own diagnostic tests or seek online specialist consultations. Others ... bypass brand name drugs for less-expensive generic and therapeutic substitutes and over-the-counter drugs. When people spend their own money, they ... generally do not spend a dollar on health care unless they get a dollar's worth of benefit.

Changes in Tax Code Are Needed to Reform Health Care

For the first time in 60 years, individually-purchased insurance and employer-purchased insurance would compete on a level playing field under the tax law.... There would literally be no reason for an employer to offer insurance (instead of wages) unless there were clear efficiencies or other advantages from group purchase.

The main reason companies today provide their workers with health insurance rather than pay higher wages is the tax law. In contrast to taxable wages, every dollar an employer spends on employee health insurance premiums avoids federal income and payroll taxes, as well as state and local income taxes. For a middle-income employee, this generous tax subsidy means that government is effectively paying for almost half the cost of the insurance. People who purchase health insurance on their own get virtually no tax relief, however. They must buy their insurance with after-tax dollars. As a result, a middle-income family effectively pays twice as much if they have to buy insurance directly.

The president proposed making premiums an above-the-line deduction (available even to taxpayers who do not itemize) for individually-purchased HSA policies. And there would be a credit to offset payroll taxes on the income used to pay premiums.

Workers who rely on their employers for health coverage have 40 percent less job mobility compared to similar workers who obtain their health coverage elsewhere.

Health Insurance Needs to Belong to Individuals, Not Employers

One of the most radical reforms the president [proposed was] to allow employers to purchase individually-owned, personal and portable insurance for their employees—insurance that would travel with them from job to job. Although few specifics are available, the genesis of this idea is a plan designed by the National Center for Policy and Blue Cross/Blue Shield of Texas. The administration [proposed] to take this idea nationwide—allowing federally regulated insurers to sell such policies in every state.

One of the peculiarities of the current system is that the health plan most of us have is not a plan that we chose; rather, it was selected by our employer. Moreover, we can easily lose coverage because of the loss of a job, a change in employment or a decision by our employer. Virtually all employer health insurance contracts last only 12 months. At the end of the year, the employer—in search of ways to reduce costs—may choose a different health plan or cease providing health insurance altogether.

All too often, a switch in health plans means changing doctors too, since each plan tends to have its own network. Additionally, different employer plans have different benefit packages. So some services, like mental health, may be covered under one employer's plan but not under the next employer's plan.

These disruptions affect some families more than others. For people who are healthy, they may amount to minor inconveniences. But if an employee (or a member of the employee's family) has a health problem, it means discontinuity of care. One study of chronically ill workers found that workers who rely on their employers for health coverage have 40 percent less job mobility compared to similar workers who obtain their health coverage elsewhere. This "job lock" can lower the potential incomes of the workers affected.

Under the president's proposal, employers initially would pay most of the premiums (as they do today). But this insurance would be owned by the employees and would travel with them as they move through the labor market. Thus employees would get portable insurance (a characteristic of individual insurance), but at group insurance prices.

Tailoring Health Care to Chronic Illness

Equally radical [was] the president's proposal to allow employers to make special deposits to the HSAs of the chronically ill. Until now, HSAs have not been designed with sick

103

people in mind. But they could be. Employers currently make different premium payments for employees, depending on their expected cost; similarly, the president's plan would allow them to deposit different amounts into their HSAs.

Studies show that with a modest amount of training, people with chronic conditions—like diabetes or asthma—can manage their own health care and achieve results at least as good as and at less cost than traditional care. If they could also manage the dollars involved, we could align financial incentives with health incentives.

For instance, if asthmatics with HSAs monitor their condition and avoid trips to the emergency room, they would not only improve their health, they would also benefit financially. Diabetics who monitor their blood glucose levels and avoid costly complications would realize financial benefits as well as health benefits from their decisions. Pilot programs for the disabled are already showing very positive results (in Medicaid, of all places!). These programs allow patients to choose some of their health care providers, and give patients an account with which to pay for health care services.

Considering that chronic patients spend about 70 percent of all health care dollars, this is not a minor reform. It is a huge reform.

These reforms ... will reshape the health care market-place by empowering patients and turning them into true consumers of care.

Free Health Insurers to Compete Nationally

In an ideal world, you would be able to go online and buy insurance in a national marketplace instead of being forced to buy in the state where you live. Thanks to the Supreme Court you can now buy wine across state lines, which has led to a big drop in costs for many consumers. When you can buy insurance the way you buy wine, insurance premium costs will plummet as well.

Many cities and towns have only one insurer. In these markets, policies are often offered on a "take it or leave it" basis. They may be overpriced, with benefits that do not fit the needs of many individuals and families. But with few or no alternatives, buyers must purchase a less desirable plan or forgo insurance altogether.

Excess Insurance Regulation Creates Excess Costs

Furthermore, state governments regulate health insurance excessively. And they do so in 50 different ways. In addition to taxes, price controls and regulations governing access to insurance, states require health insurance buyers to pay for extra benefits they may not want or need. Studies estimate that as many as one out of every four uninsured Americans has been priced out of the health insurance market by these regulations and mandated benefits.

The president [proposed] to allow insurers licensed in any one state to sell insurance in every other state under the rules and regulations of the home state. This is a major step in the direction of replacing 50 over-regulated markets with one large, relatively free and less-costly market.

A New Health Care Vision

All of these reforms will make health insurance more affordable and more accessible. They will reshape the health care marketplace by empowering patients and turning them into true consumers of care. They will strengthen the doctor-patient relationship and allow doctors to be agents of their patients rather than agents of third-party payers. All in all, they are a vast improvement over the current system.

Deregulating Health Care Can Make Services More Affordable

Christopher J. Conover

About the author: *Christopher J. Conover, Ph.D., is an assistant research professor at the Center for Health Policy, Law and Management and Director of the Health Policy Certificate Program at Duke University in Durham, North Carolina. His research interests include health policy and economics, medical care for people who are medically indigent and/or uninsured, health care reform and regulation, and state health policies.*

Students of regulation have known for decades that the burden of regulation on the U.S. economy is sizable, with the latest figures suggesting this cost may approach $1 trillion in 2004. Surprisingly, given that the health industry is often viewed as among the most heavily regulated sectors of the U.S. economy, previous estimates generally have ignored the cost of regulating health care services.

The High Cost of Health Services Regulation

Using a "top-down" approach, one can arrive at a "back-of-the-envelope" estimate that health services regulation imposes an annual cost of $256 billion per year (with a range of $28 billion to $657 billion), suggesting that health services regulations could increase estimates of overall regulatory costs by more than 25 percent.

A far more accurate "bottom-up" approach suggests that the total cost of health services regulation exceeds $339.2 billion. This figure takes into account regulation of health facilities, health professionals, health insurance, drugs and medical devices, and the medical tort system, including the costs of defensive medicine. Moreover, this approach allows for a calculation of some important tangible benefits of regulation. Yet even after subtracting $170.1 billion in benefits, the net burden of health services regulation is considerable, amounting to $169.1 billion annually. In other words, the costs of health services regulation outweigh benefits by two-to-one and cost the average household over $1,500 per year.

The high cost of health services regulation is responsible for more than seven million Americans lacking health insurance, or one in six of the average daily uninsured. Moreover, 4,000 more Americans die every year from costs associated with health services regulation (22,000) than from lack of health insurance (18,000). The annual net cost of health services regulation dwarfs other costs imposed by government intervention in the health care sector. This cost exceeds annual consumer expenditures on gasoline and oil in the United States and is twice the size of the annual output of the motion picture and sound recording industries.

Spread across all households, health services regulation cost the average household an estimated $1,546 in 2002.

Routes to Reform

Finding ways to reduce or eliminate this excess cost should be an urgent priority for policymakers. It would appear from this preliminary assessment that medical tort reform offers the most promising target for regulatory cost savings, followed by FDA [the federal Food and Drug Administration] reform, selected access-oriented health insurance regulations (e.g., mandated health benefits), and quality-oriented health facilities regulations (e.g., accreditation and licensure). . . .

All told, these access-related facilities regulations as a group cost $11.8 billion but provide benefits of only $3.8 billion. Hospital uncompensated care pools (net cost $5.2 billion) and EMTALA (net cost $2.3 billion account for the lion's share of this net cost. . . .

Total Cost of Health Services Regulation

When estimates across all five major categories of regulation are combined, the expected costs of regulation in health care amounted to $339.2 billion in 2002. Benefits are estimated to be $170.1 billion, leaving a net cost of $169.1 billion. Three areas account for the lion's share of this net burden. The cost of the medical tort system, including litigation costs, court expenses, and defensive medicine, totals $80.6 billion. FDA regulation adds another $41.9 billion, and health facilities regulation adds $25.1 billion. That suggests that the states and federal government both have important roles to play in finding ways to trim regulatory excess. . . .

Benchmarks of Comparison

Health care regulatory costs should be put into context. In terms of GDP [gross domestic product] $169 billion represents 1.8 percent—roughly the relative size of the Medicare program in 1989 and more than the federal share of the Medicaid program ($148 billion), as well as total corporate tax collections ($148 billion), and the budget deficit ($158 billion) in 2002. This is comparable to the gross state products of seven states: Alaska, Idaho, Montana, North Dakota, South Dakota, Vermont, and Wyoming (combined gross state products: $174 billion in 2001). It also represents more than U.S. consumers spend on gasoline and oil ($165.8 billion in 2002) and double the output of the motion picture and sound recording industries ($81.8 billion in 2002). Spread across all households, health services regulation cost the average household an estimated $1,546 in 2002. Assuming the net annual cost of health services regulation remains constant, it will exceed by a factor of three the $534 billion that will be required to fund the new Medicare prescription drug benefit over the next 10 years, and will exceed the revenue necessary to eradicate Medicare's financial imbalances over the next 75 years.

Other Regulatory Costs Not Included Here

Health services regulation adds to—and often dwarfs—other costs imposed by government intervention in the health care sector. For example, this analysis has ignored tax policy as it relates to health care. Yet federal and state tax subsidies for health insurance in 2002 amounted to an estimated $177 billion and generated roughly $106 billion in efficiency losses—an amount that would increase the estimate of the cost of health services regulation by three-fifths had it been included. On a smaller scale, a recent study of Medicare found that $26 billion of Medicare expenditures in 1996 (equivalent to $34 billion in 2002) is wasted ("appears to provide no benefit in terms of survival, nor is it likely that this extra spending improves the quality of life"). This does not even count the presumably much greater amount of care that may confer some medical benefit, but which has a value to patients is less than the cost of its provision. Nor does it count the amount of such waste in Medicaid, the State Children's Health Insurance Program, or other government health programs. Thus, there are clearly areas apart from health services regulatory costs where Americans could get more bang for the buck. . . .

The potential savings from regulatory reform in health services are far too great to be ignored.

The pressures to regulate are unrelenting. . . .

More than a decade ago, some pioneers in estimating regulatory costs stated, "We believe that improving and disseminating better information is likely to induce decision-makers to scrutinize the costs and benefits of regulation more carefully. We hope that this increased care will lead to more efficient decisions." The estimates in this report, as uncertain and incomplete as they may be, have been assembled with the same motivation.

Prioritizing the Reform of Health Services Regulation

In terms of priorities, it would appear from this preliminary assessment that medical tort reform offers the most promising target for regulatory cost savings, followed by FDA reform, selected access-oriented health insurance regulations (e.g., mandated health benefits), and quality-oriented health facilities regulations (e.g., accreditation and licensure). . . . What should be clear from even this rough picture of the health services regulatory landscape is that the potential savings from regulatory reform in health services are far too great to be ignored.

Medicaid Should Be Restructured So the Poor and Weakest Can Buy Whatever Health Care They Choose

Jeffrey M. Jones

About the author*: Jeffrey M. Jones is a research fellow at the Hoover Institution, a conservative think tank at Stanford University in Palo Alto, California.*

An important debate surfaced in the wake of Hurricane Katrina [2005] that could lead to a shift in social policy as significant as the welfare reform law of 1996. The devastation wrought by the hurricane in Louisiana, Mississippi, and parts of Alabama left many already poor people even more destitute. The nation's sense of compassion was stirred, and thousands of volunteers and millions of charitable dollars flowed into affected areas. After initial missteps, the federal response intensified as President [George W.] Bush and congressional leaders pledged significant resources to the region. . . .

The questions raised [by Hurricane Katrina] about how best to meet the health-care needs of the poor may have unexpectedly introduced the nation to its next major welfare reform target.

The Write-Up on Medicaid

Medicaid was enacted as part of the Social Security Amendments of 1965 to assist states in providing adequate medical care to eligible needy persons. It started at the same time as its sister program, Medicare, which offers health insurance to the elderly. Medicaid was gradually phased in on a state-by-state basis between 1966 and 1972. Unlike Medicare, in which the federal government provides all the funding, Medicaid is jointly financed by the federal government and the states. In its first year, the combined expenditures totaled $1.7 billion, with the states paying just over half the costs. In 1972, with 49 of the 50 states on board. Medicaid spending had increased to $8.4 billion, covering a total enrollment of 17.6 million adults and children.

Every state operates a Medicaid system . . . characterized by price controls and . . . defined benefits. Together, these factors create inflexibility and fewer choices for beneficiaries.

Medicaid serves a diverse population that includes foster-care children, mothers on welfare, and elderly nursing home residents. Although three-quarters of its beneficiaries are low-income women and children, together they only account for one-third of the spending on health care, meaning that the relatively smaller populations of aged and blind/disabled Medicaid recipients account for the lion's share of medical expenses. This makes sense when one considers the high cost of personalized disability services and long-term nursing home care. According to a report by the National Bureau of Economic Research, "This panoply of functions has led to uneven program growth and some confusion about the mission of the program and how it integrates with other public insurance institutions."

Adding to the confusion, each state is responsible for designing and administering its own program. Within federal guidelines, states determine eligibility requirements, program benefits, and reimbursements to health care providers. The result is a patchwork of medical services and coverage that varies from state to state. Despite these differences, every state operates a Medicaid system that is characterized by price controls and a package of defined benefits. Together, these factors create inflexibility and fewer choices for beneficiaries.

Medicaid dwarfs . . . other major means-tested programs, . . . [rising] steadily [in] . . . the federal budget . . . from approximately 4 percent in 1975 to 13 percent in 2002.

A 40-Year Growth Spurt

Since its inception, Medicaid enrollments and spending have grown rapidly. That growth is in part a reflection of the rise in health-care costs nationally but is also a result of states' loosening their eligibility requirements, resulting in more and more recipients. . . .

In terms of expenditures, Medicaid dwarfs the other major means-tested programs. Spending on Medicaid has risen steadily as a fraction of the federal budget during each of the past three decades, increasing from approximately 4 percent in 1975 to 13 percent in 2002. That year, total outlays for the Medicaid program (federal and state) were $259 billion, or an average of $4,291 per recipient. And the costs are projected to continue to rise. "Medicaid—not Medicare—is now the largest government health program in the United States," according to the programs' administrator, Thomas Scully. "This trend is continuing," he says, "with Medicaid outlays exceeding Medicare by about $4 billion in FY [fiscal year] 2003 ($281 billion versus $277 billion), and estimated to exceed it by approximately $26 billion in FY 2004 ($304 billion versus $289 billion)."

Spending increases have contributed to the recent federal budget deficit. [In 2005] President Bush asked Congress to cut as much as $10 billion over five years from the federal portion of Medicaid's budget. Of even greater concern is the impact rising costs are having on state budgets. Medicaid expenditures alone account for approximately 22 percent of all state spending, and more than half the states exceeded their Medicaid budgets in FY 2005. Many state constitutions require a balanced budget; thus the Medicaid cost overruns must be covered by either raising taxes or cutting spending in other areas such as education, law enforcement, or transportation. Without question, rising Medicaid costs pose the single greatest risk to state financing and solvency.

An Ailing System of Care

The fiscal crisis is the most obvious trauma threatening the Medicaid entitlement. But the immediacy of such concerns should not draw attention away from persistent quality-of-care and administrative problems. Public surveys confirm the commonsense conclusion that most Americans would rather have private health insurance than Medicaid. One reason is the dearth of doctors willing to treat Medicaid patients—according to one survey, 4 in 10 physicians have such restrictions. Additionally, cost-containment measures currently being implemented lead to rationing health care by means of restricted formularies and monthly limits on prescription drugs. Provider payments are being reduced, rules on eligibility and benefits are being tightened, and states are introducing co-pays to share costs. Each of these measures affects the quality and availability of care, producing a two-tiered health system that stigmatizes and harms the poor. Not surprisingly, dissatisfaction with Medicaid is common among recipients.

When Hurricane Katrina hit land on August 29, 2005, it exposed a lot more than the poor urban planning and antiquated levees of New Orleans.

Administratively, Medicaid has endured years of mismanagement, abuse, and outright fraud. From health officials failing to secure prescription drug discounts to insurance scams designed to collect fees for phony treatments, problems abound. A major flaw in the design of Medicaid is the Federal Medical Assistance Percentage (FMAP), or federal match, which has been shown in studies and congressional testimony to encourage "a variety of legal and regulatory loopholes to enhance the Federal funds [states] receive." When the feds chip in two or three dollars for every dollar spent by the states on Medicaid services, the incentives to increase spending or expand the definition of "Medicaid services" are clear. The Center for Medicare & Medicaid Services (CMS) has recently taken steps to rein in such abuse and has made strengthening financial oversight a top priority. Although eliminating "gamesmanship" is important for government accountability, it will certainly exacerbate the trade-offs between state financial solvency and the quality/availability of care for Medicaid beneficiaries.

Right Diagnosis, Wrong Prescription

When Hurricane Katrina hit land on August 29, 2005, it exposed a lot more than the poor urban planning and antiquated levees of New Orleans. In President Bush's words, "As all of us saw on television, there's also some deep, persistent poverty in this region," with "roots in a history of racial discrimination."

Among the first tasks to confront was providing health care to the victims of Katrina. Within weeks of the disaster, two approaches began to take shape. On September 15, Senators [Charles] Grassley and [Max] Baucus introduced a bill (S. 1716) titled the Emergency Health Care Relief Act of 2005. The $8.7 billion proposal principally alters Medicaid rules so as to provide relief to hurricane survivors and the affected states for an initial five months. The bill [sought] to expand eligibility to women and children with incomes up to 200 percent of the federal poverty line, as well as childless men previously barred from Medicaid. Benefits were also enhanced, with generous coverage of treatments for emotional and psychological disorders resulting from Hurricane Katrina and extension of TANF [Temporary Assistance for Needy Families, a federal program] benefits and unemployment compensation. Furthermore, S. 1716 [absolved] the states of paying for any of the Medicaid expenses incurred by eligible evacuees—eliminating the state match and reimbursing, from the federal treasury, 100 percent of the costs.

The second approach, championed by Health and Human Services Secretary Mike Leavitt on behalf of the Bush administration, involved granting waivers on a state-by-state basis. The waivers [made] it easier for states to meet the health-care needs of individuals enrolled in Medicare, Medicaid, and the State Children's Health Insurance Program. Enrollees evacuated to other states [would] continue to be covered, and the standards for eligibility [were] simplified to get health care to as many qualified evacuees as possible. In addition, cost-sharing and mandatory managed care [were] suspended for evacuees and extra mental health benefits [were] available. For individuals not covered through private or public health insurance programs, CMS [funded] an "uncompensated care pool" to reimburse providers for services rendered to uninsured evacuees. One significant advantage [was] that Secretary Leavitt [had] the authority to grant waivers and [had] already reached agreements covering such waivers with Alabama, Florida, Georgia, Louisiana, Mississippi, and Texas, among others.

Following in the footsteps of welfare reform, Medicaid can be restructured to increase personal responsibility and enhance individual freedom.

Objections to the Grassley/Baucus approach [included] its high costs, entitlement expansion to childless adults, and delays in implementing planned reforms to FMAP. Criticisms of the Bush administration approach [included] some evacuees having been turned down for Medicaid, an inadequately funded uncompensated care pool, and Louisiana, Mississippi, and Alabama being unable to afford their portion of Medicaid expenditures, which [were] expected to be well above historical averages.

Whatever the shortcomings of the state waiver remedy, the risks involved in expanding Medicaid through legislation far outweighed them. Despite 40-plus years of massive government entitlement spending to eliminate poverty, Katrina revealed just how little progress has been made. Instead of breaking the cycle of poverty, entitlements such as Medicaid reinforce government dependency. Out-of-control costs, fraud, abuse, and poor quality of care point to a system on the brink of failure. The survivors of Hurricane Katrina deserve better. The short-term payoff of a $9 billion aid package is a bet our country cannot afford to make. Ultimately, the problems with Medicaid and the limitations of the federal waiver plan can only serve to heighten, as President Bush put it, our "duty to confront this poverty with bold action."

New Treatments Offer Hope

If a new Medicaid entitlement is out of the question and federal waivers come up short, what "bold action" can we take? Following in the footsteps of welfare reform, Medicaid can be restructured to increase personal responsibility and enhance individual freedom. Our best option for securing and improving the physical welfare of impoverished Americans is to move away from a system of socialized health care. In its place, federal and state governments can use their financial resources to help the poor afford private medical insurance and services tailored to their specific needs.

Inevitably, detractors will argue that such a "scheme" is too risky and will hurt the poor while lining the pockets of wealthy private insurance corporations. The charges are always the same—vague and combative. But the facts say otherwise.

A remarkable demonstration project is under way in several states called the Cash and Counseling Program. Under this program, certain disabled and older beneficiaries are able to purchase community-based care and home health services with cash allowances. They can shop around, hire and fire, and generally have their disability needs met on their time schedule and as they see fit. This dramatically alters the benefits structure of Medicaid in favor of the consumer's interests. Benefits are no longer defined by bureaucrats but by those actually using the health services.

The results have pleased both the beneficiaries and the states, something Medicaid has failed to do on both counts. In Florida, an evaluation by Mathematica [a policy research company specializing in health care] found that satisfaction among program participants is extremely high—99 percent were satisfied with their caregivers, 88 percent said that their quality of life had improved, and 97 percent would recommend the program. In addition to beneficiary satisfaction, the program has energized states by significantly reducing fraud and abuse and offering a way out of the annual growth in spending. The Cash and Counseling Program utilizes a defined contribution model that caps state expenditures. This prevents the program from going over budget and introduces incentives that encourage beneficiaries to spend wisely on their routine care. And there is a promise of additional fiscal savings for states as consumers opt for home care over more costly institutionalized care.

Cash and Counseling, although demonstrating the potential of consumer-directed health care, is designed for individuals with various types of disabilities and illnesses. For the vast majority of Medicaid recipients, a more simplified option is gaining traction. Premium support programs can take several forms, but all essentially give Medicaid beneficiaries the choice of receiving a financial contribution that can be used to purchase private health insurance. This approach is already being utilized in some states to help qualifying beneficiaries pay the premiums on their employer-sponsored health plans. . . .

The problems that plague Medicaid, including cost overruns, reduced benefits, and restrictions on eligibility, will not go away on their own. . . . Ideas have consequences, and those that have propped up the failing Medicaid system will continue [to] be voiced. The question is, "Can we afford to listen any longer?"

Consumer-Driven Health Plans Are Not Effective

Paul Fronstin and Sara R. Collins

About the authors: *Paul Fronstin is Senior Research Associate, and Director of the Health Security and Quality Research Program at the Washington, D.C., Employee Benefit Research Institute, a research organization focused on developing sound employee benefit programs and public policy. Sara R. Collins is an assistant vice-president of the Future of Health Insurance at the Commonwealth Fund, a liberal foundation focused on health care. She was previously an associate director/senior research associate at the New York Academy of Medicine.*

Promoting consumerism in health care is the latest big idea in health insurance in the United States. One of the leading manifestations of this is the use of high-deductible health plans (HDHPs) with savings accounts, such as health savings accounts (HSAs) and health reimbursement arrangements (HRAs), collectively known as consumer-driven health plans (CDHPs).

The first EBRI [Employee Benefit Research Institute]/ Commonwealth Fund Consumerism in Health Care Survey was conducted to provide reliable national data on the growth of high deductible plans and their impact on the behavior and attitudes of health care consumers. The study defines high-deductible plans as those that would qualify for federal HSA tax preferences: with deductibles of $1,000 or more for individual plans and $2,000 or more for family plans. Survey findings indicate:

- *Lower satisfaction with consumer-driven plans.* The EBRI/Commonwealth Fund Consumerism in Health Care Survey—the first national survey of its kind— found that individuals with more comprehensive health insurance were more satisfied with their health plan than individuals in high deductible plans, with or without accounts. Specifically, 63 percent of individuals with comprehensive health insurance were extremely or very satisfied with their health plan, compared with 42 percent of CDHP enrollees and 33 percent of HDHP participants. About 60 percent of individuals with comprehensive insurance reported they were extremely or very likely to stay with their current health plan if they had the opportunity to switch, compared with 46 percent of CDHP enrollees and 30 percent of HDHP enrollees.

- *Higher out-of-pocket costs.* Despite similar rates of health care use, individuals with CDHPs and HDHPs are significantly more likely to spend a large share of their income on out-of-pocket health care expenses than those in comprehensive health plans. Two-fifths (42 percent) of those in HDHPs and 31 percent of those in CDHPs spent 5 percent or more of their income on out-of pocket costs and premiums in the last year, compared with 12 percent of those in more comprehensive health plans.

- *More missed health care.* Individuals with CDHPs and HDHPs were significantly more likely to avoid, skip, or delay health care because of costs than were those with more comprehensive health insurance, with problems particularly pronounced among those with health problems or incomes under $50,000. About one-third of individuals in CHDPs (35 percent) and HDHPs (31 percent) reported delaying or avoiding care, compared with 17 percent of those in comprehensive health plans.

- *More cost-conscious consumers.* Among people in the plans who did receive care, there is evidence that they are more cost-conscious than those in comprehensive health plans. People in the CDHPs and HDHPs were significantly more likely to say that the terms of their health plans made them consider costs when deciding to see a doctor when sick or fill a prescription, to report that they had checked whether their health plan would cover their costs as well as the price of a service prior to receiving care, and to discuss treatment options and the cost of care with their doctors. Nevertheless, they were also more likely to go without care.

- *Lack of information.* Few health plans of any type provide cost and quality information about providers to help people make informed decisions about their health care. The study also found very low levels of trust in information provided by health plans.

Consumer-Driven Health Plans Erode Health Care for All Americans

Paul Krugman and Robin Wells

About the authors: *Paul Krugman is a columnist for the* New York Times *and teaches at the Woodrow Wilson School of Public and International Affairs at Princeton University in Princeton, New Jersey. Robin Wells is the coauthor (with Paul Krugman) of* Economics *(2006).*

[In 1993] Bill Clinton became president partly because he promised to do something about rising health care costs. Although Clinton's chances of reforming the US health care system looked quite good at first, the effort soon ran aground. Since then a combination of factors—the unwillingness of other politicians to confront the insurance and other lobbies that so successfully frustrated the Clinton effort, a temporary remission in the growth of health care spending as HMOs [Health Maintenance Organizations] briefly managed to limit cost increases, and the general distraction of a nation focused first on the gloriousness of getting rich, then on terrorism—have kept health care off the top of the agenda.

But medical costs are once again rising rapidly, forcing health care back into political prominence. . . .

Some Background on Employer-Provided Health Insurance

Providing health insurance looked like a good way for employers to reward their employees when it was a small part of the pay package. Today, however, the annual cost of coverage

Paul Krugman and Robin Wells, "The Health Care Crisis and What to Do About It," *New York Review of Books*, vol. 53, March 23, 2006, pp. 38–43. Copyright © 2006 by NYREV, Inc. Reprinted with permission from The New York Review of Books.

for a family of four is estimated by the Kaiser Family Foundation at more than $10,000. One way to look at it is to say that that's roughly what a worker earning minimum wage and working full time earns in a year. It's more than half the annual earnings of the average Wal-Mart employee.

Health care costs at current levels override the incentives that have historically supported employer-based health insurance. Now that health costs loom so large, companies that provide generous benefits are in effect paying some of their workers much more than the going wage—or, more to the point, more than competitors pay similar workers. Inevitably, this creates pressure to reduce or eliminate health benefits. And companies that can't cut benefits enough to stay competitive—such as GM [General Motors]—find their very existence at risk.

Rising health costs have also ended the ability of employer-based insurance plans to avoid the problem of adverse selection. Anecdotal evidence suggests that workers who know they have health problems actively seek out jobs with companies that still offer generous benefits. On the other side, employers are starting to make hiring decisions based on likely health costs. For example, an internal Wal-Mart memo, reported by *The New York Times* in October, suggested adding tasks requiring physical exertion to jobs that don't really require it as a way to screen out individuals with potential health risks.

The underlying view behind the Bush administration's health care proposals [is] the view that insurance leads people to consume too much health care.

So rising health care costs are undermining the institution of employer-based coverage. We'd suggest that the drop in the number of insured so far only hints at the scale of the problem: we may well be seeing the whole institution unraveling. . . .

How Much Is Too Much Health Insurance?

We've already alluded to the underlying view behind the [George W.] Bush administration's health care proposals: it's the view that insurance leads people to consume too much health care. The 2004 *Economic Report of the President*, which devoted a chapter to health care, illustrated the alleged problem with a parable about the clothing industry:

> Suppose, for example, that an individual could purchase a clothing insurance policy with a "coinsurance" rate of 20 percent, meaning that after paying the insurance premium, the holder of the insurance policy would have to pay only 20 cents on the dollar for all clothing purchases. An individual with such a policy would be expected to spend substantially more on clothes—due to larger quantity and higher quality purchases—with the 80 percent discount than he would at the full price.... The clothing insurance example suggests an inherent inefficiency in the use of insurance to pay for things that have little intrinsic risk or uncertainty.

The report then asserts that "inefficiencies of this sort are pervasive in the US health care system"—although, tellingly, it fails to match the parable about clothing with any real examples from health care.

The view that Americans consume too much health care because insurers pay the bills leads to what is currently being called the "consumer-directed" approach to health care reform. The virtues of such an approach are the theme of John Cogan, Glenn Hubbard, and Daniel Kessler's *Healthy, Wealthy, and Wise* (2005). The main idea is that people should pay more of their medical expenses out of pocket. And the way to reduce public reliance on insurance, reformers from the right wing believe, is to remove the tax advantages that currently favor health insurance over out-of-pocket spending. Indeed, last year Bush's tax reform commission proposed taxing some employment-based health benefits. The administration, recognizing how politically explosive such a move would be, rejected the proposal. Instead of raising taxes on health insurance, the administration has decided to cut taxes on out-of-pocket spending.

Health savings accounts, whatever their ostensible goals, are yet another tax break for the wealthy, who have already been showered with tax breaks.

Cogan, Hubbard, and Kessler call for making all out-of-pocket medical spending tax-deductible, although tax experts from both parties say that this would present an enforcement nightmare. (Douglas Holtz-Eakin, the former head of the Congressional Budget Office, put it this way: "If you want to have a personal relationship with the IRS do that [i.e., make all medical spending tax deductible] because we are going to have to investigate everybody's home to see if their running shoes are a medical expense.") The administration's proposals so far are more limited, focusing on an expanded system of tax-advantaged health savings accounts. Individuals can shelter part of their income from taxes by depositing it in such accounts, then withdraw money from these accounts to pay medical bills.

The Problems with Consumer-Directed Health Care

What's wrong with consumer-directed health care? One immediate disadvantage is that health savings accounts, whatever their ostensible goals, are yet another tax break for the wealthy, who have already been showered with tax breaks under Bush. The right to pay medical expenses with pre-tax income is worth a lot to high-income individuals who face a marginal income tax rate of 35 percent, but little or nothing to lower-income Americans who face a marginal tax rate of 10 percent or less, and lack the ability to place the maximum allowed amount in their savings accounts.

A deeper disadvantage is that such accounts tend to undermine employment-based health care, because they encourage adverse selection: health savings accounts are attractive to healthier individuals, who will be tempted to opt out of company plans, leaving less healthy individuals behind.

The administration's plans for consumer-directed health care . . . are a diversion from meaningful health care reform, and will actually worsen our health care problems.

Yet another problem with consumer-directed care is that the evidence says that people don't, in fact, make wise decisions when paying for medical care out of pocket. A classic study by the RAND Corporation found that when people pay medical expenses themselves rather than relying on insurance, they do cut back on their consumption of health care—but that they cut back on valuable as well as questionable medical procedures, showing no ability to set sensible priorities.

Who Pays for Routine Care?

But perhaps the biggest objection to consumer-directed health reform is that its advocates have misdiagnosed the problem. They believe that Americans have too much health insurance; the 2004 *Economic Report of the President* condemned the fact that insurance currently pays for "many events that have little uncertainty, such as routine dental care, annual medical exams, and vaccinations," and for "relatively low-expense items, such as an office visit to the doctor for a sore throat." The implication is that health costs are too high because people who don't pay their own medical bills consume too much routine dental care and are too ready to visit the doctor about a sore throat. And that argument is all wrong. Excessive consumption of routine care, or small-expense items, can't be a major source of health care inefficiency, because such items don't account for a major share of medical costs.

Remember the 80-20 rule: the great bulk of medical expenses are accounted for by a small number of people requiring very expensive treatment. When you think of the problem of health care costs, you shouldn't envision visits to the family physician to talk about a sore throat; you should think about coronary bypass operations, dialysis, and chemotherapy. Nobody is proposing a consumer-directed health care plan that would force individuals to pay a large share of extreme medical expenses, such as the costs of chemotherapy, out of pocket. And that means that consumer-directed health care can't promote savings on the treatments that account for most of what we spend on health care.

The administration's plans for consumer-directed health care, then, are a diversion from meaningful health care reform, and will actually worsen our health care problems.

Consumer-Driven Health Care Will Not Eliminate the High Costs of Private Care

Hendrik Hertzberg

About the author: *Hendrik Hertzberg has been the executive editor of the literary magazine* The New Yorker *since 1992. He was editor of the liberal political magazine* The New Republic *from 1981 to 1985 and from 1988 to 1991. During U.S. president Jimmy Carter's administration, Mr. Hertzberg served on the White House staff as President Carter's speech writer (1979–1981).*

Perhaps you have been wondering who or what is to blame for the high cost of medical care in this land of ours—and, more broadly, for the ungainly, unjust mess that is the American health-care system. If so, wonder no more. Your government has fingered the culprit: it's "the vast majority of Americans."

The perp having been collared, the trial held, and the verdict rendered, only the sentencing phase remains. Providentially, our leaders have come up with a punishment that fits the crime. We, the guilty, are to be condemned—or invited, but in any case for the rest of our natural lives, without possibility of parole—to turn over our bodily well-being to "consumer-directed Health Savings Accounts" in conjunction with "high-deductible health policies."

This judgment was handed down [on April 3, 2006] in the form of an article on the Op-Ed page of the *New York Times*. The piece was no Dowdy jestfest or Friedmanesque memo-to-the-mullahs [Maureen Dowd and Thomas Friedman are liberal *New York Times* columnists] and not only because of the

Hendrik Hertzberg, "Consumption," *The New Yorker*, April 17, 2006, pp. 25–26. Copyright © 2006 by the author. All rights reserved. Reproduced by permission.

dreariness of its style and the banality of its content. Its author, Allan B. Hubbard, identified as "assistant to the president for economic policy and director of the National Economic Council," has lately emerged as the [George W. Bush] White House point man on health policy, and, in subsequent days, his Op-Ed proved to have been the overture to a veritable symphony of spin conducted by President Bush himself, including an Air Force One ride to Bridgeport, Connecticut, for a stagy "Panel on Health Savings Accounts."

Can this really be the Administration's view of the health-care crisis? . . . That we're over *insured?*

Hubbard's article, headlined "THE HEALTH OF A NATION," begins with a frank-sounding acknowledgment that "in the past five years"—that is, since the present Administration took office—"private health insurance premiums have risen 73 percent," with the result that "some businesses" have dropped coverage altogether. "What is driving this unsustainable run-up in health insurance costs," Hubbard asks, "and how can we make things better?" Then comes what bloggers call the money quote:

> Health care is expensive because the vast majority of Americans consume it as if it were free. Health insurance policies with low deductibles insulate people from the cost of the medical care they use—so much so that they often do not even ask for prices.

Can this really be the Administration's view of the health-care crisis? That its root cause is that Americans are (a) malingerers and (b) freeloaders who perversely refuse to go comparison shopping when illness strikes? That we're *over* insured? Hard as it is to believe that this is what they say, it's even harder to believe that this is what they believe.

Why Health Care Is So Expensive

Health care is indeed expensive, but not because people are too quick to call the doctor when they experience a scary symptom or merely an annoying one, and not because some of them may bridle at entrusting their health to the lowest bidder. Throughout the Western world, health care is expensive, first of all, because it is expensive, and is bound to get more so as populations age and medical technology advances. Indeed, it *should* get more expensive, both in absolute terms and as a proportion of national income, because what it aims to provide—healing, the relief of suffering, the staving off of death—is of such inestimable value.

American health care is the most expensive on earth, but this, too, has little to do with overindulgence in seeking medical attention. (Overindulgence in cheeseburgers is another matter.) It has a lot to do with the waste built into what Paul Krugman [another liberal *New York Times* columnist and an economist] calls our crazy-quilt health-care system, which has a lot to do with the fact that so much of that system is private rather than public, which in turn has a lot to do with two other factors. One is historical: during the Second World War, industry (with prodding from organized labor) got around wage controls by offering workers health benefits in place of cash, thus saddling the United States with "employer-based" private health insurance—a system now in slow-motion collapse under the competitive pressures of globalization. The other is institutional: even though there has long been popular support here for universal, government-run health care, as there is in Europe and Canada, America's fragmented political system—riddled with weak points where well-organized, well-financed minorities can thwart the unfocussed will of a majority—has been able to deliver only for seniors and, less generously, for the poor.

Public Health Care Has Lower Administrative Expenses Than Private Care

Medicare—a mixed system, under which the insurance function is socialized while the care itself remains in private hands—dedicates two per cent of its resources to administration. By contrast, the private health-insurance industry spends a fortune—more than ten per cent of its income—on administrative dreadnoughts devoted largely to vetoing treatments, sloughing off sick or potentially sick clients, and scheming to stick someone else with the bill. In the United States, we spend fifteen per cent of our gross domestic product [G.D.P.] on health care, close to six thousand dollars per person. The French and the Canadians spend ten per cent of G.D.P., about three thousand dollars per head. Yet their "health outcomes," measured by indices like longevity, are better than ours. If they spent the kind of money we do, they'd live forever.

The Fallacy of a Consumer Marketplace for Health

Hubbard—who, by the way, is a finalist to be Bush's next Secretary of the Treasury—is an initiate of the cult of the market, which he evidently regards as the fundamental model for all human relations. For him, sick people who require care are "consumers." That word and its derivatives appear ten times in the eight hundred and fifty words of his *Times* piece. ("Patient" appears once. "Sick," "ill," and "under the weather" do not appear at all.) Accordingly, the solution that he and Bush are pushing—so-called health savings accounts—puts the onus on "consumers" to fend for themselves in the medical "marketplace." It's probably unnecessary to add that this solution would solve nothing. It would be yet another gift to people in the higher tax brackets, would undermine traditional insurance by pulling young and healthy people out of risk pools, and, with a fine evenhandedness, would discourage people from going to the doctor for real and imaginary illnesses alike. This is a worthy follow-up to the Administration's prescription-drug program for seniors, another excrescence of market cultism. The elderly had hoped for a straightforward benefit that would have allowed them to acquire, at some affordable price, the medicines their doctors prescribed. What they got was a parody of "choice," sadistic in its complexity, which forces them or their children or caretakers to game out which of dozens of private "plans" might give them access both to the medicines they need now and the ones they might unpredictably need in the future. The solicitude their government might have bestowed on them was reserved instead for the insurance and pharmaceutical industries. The Administration's message to the old and sick is the same as its message to the country after the September 11th attacks: Go shopping. Well, caveat emptor.

Consumer-Driven Health Plans Do Not Provide Equal and Sufficient Information for Making Informed Medical Decisions

Cheryl Damberg

About the author: *Cheryl Damberg is a senior policy researcher at the RAND Corporation, one of the United States' oldest public policy, research, and analysis think tanks. The nonpartisan organization is headquartered in Santa Monica, California.*

Consumer-Directed Health Plans [CDHPs] involve increased incentives to make consumers financially responsible when they choose costly health care options. The design of these plan models is predicated on the assumption that consumers will seek and use information on the efficacy of treatment and provider performance if they have a sizeable financial stake in care decisions. Employers hope that by providing consumers with informational tools and financial incentives, this approach will work to contain the growth in health care costs by inducing consumers to eliminate unnecessary care and to seek lower-cost, higher quality providers.

Consumer-Directed Health Plan models refer to two basic models: 1) high deductible plans that are often paired with a personal health care spending account—either a Health Reimbursement Account (HRA) or a Health Savings Account (HSA) to pay for unreimbursed medical expenditures; and 2) tiered benefit designs—either "tiered premium" plans that require high patient cost sharing if a consumer selects a less-restrictive network of providers (either hospitals, physicians, or both) or

Cheryl Damberg, "Consumer-Directed Health Plans: Research on Implications for Health Care Quality and Cost," RAND Corporation, September 2005. Copyright © 2005 Rand Corporation. Reprinted by permission.

"tiered-provider" plans, where a consumer pays lower costs when selecting a provider in a preferred tier. . . .

Estimated Cost Benefits of High-Deductible Health Insurance

The results of the RAND Health Insurance Experiment [HIE], a randomized controlled trial of the effects of cost sharing on health care use conducted between 1974 and 1982, have been used to simulate the effect of moving employees from a typical health plan to one with a high deductible. These studies suggest that moving everyone from a plan with today's typical cost-sharing features to a high-deductible plan would result in a one-time reduction in spending of about 4–15%. These estimates are based on a shift to high-deductible only plans without personal savings accounts; personal savings accounts may mitigate to some degree the impact of the financial incentive to the consumer and thus offset some of these savings. Moreover, it is not known whether high deductibles will constrain the rate of growth in spending over time or just lead to a one-time reduction in spending. There is evidence that most of the growth in spending can be attributed to technological innovation, and there is little evidence that greater cost sharing will slow the adoption of new technology.

Today's plan designs may impose a greater burden on low-income families . . . and . . . may augment disparities in access to care between low- and high-income families.

In the RAND HIE, the effect of cost sharing was on the patient decision to initiate care; the amount of pending per episode of care did not vary substantially with cost sharing. However, a change in coverage for the entire population might affect practice norms among physicians (i.e., change physician behavior), leading to even greater reductions in health care use. On the other hand, some economists believe that reductions in demand for visits by patients will lead to physician-induced demand for care in an effort to offset income losses, which could somewhat offset the effects on use and spending estimated from the HIE. Thus, it remains uncertain whether large-scale changes in benefit design would lead to larger or smaller effects in total health care use and spending than found in the HIE. And, while the HIE found no difference between the poor and non-poor in the effect of increased cost sharing on health care use, today's plan designs may impose a greater burden on low-income families than was the case with the HIE, and thus may augment disparities in access to care between low- and high-income families. Additional research is required to understand the effect of cost sharing on use of care and spending given the new design features of high deductible plans, and how these effects may differ by population subgroups.

What Do We Know About the Effects of High Deductible Plans on Quality and Health?

While the RAND HIE found that greater patient cost sharing reduced use, it also concluded that the reduction generally was at the expense of care that is considered efficacious as well as less effective services, with a few exceptions. Cost sharing reduced the use of the emergency rooms for less urgent problems to a greater extent than for urgent problems, and it did not reduce use of care regarded as highly effective for non-poor children.

Lower use of services among persons with greater cost sharing in the HIE did not generally translate into adverse health effects, suggesting that the new high deductible plans would not lead to poorer health outcomes. However, negative consequences did occur for some low-income people in poor health. If new health plan designs place greater cost burdens on the low-income population than did the HIE plans, they may have broader health consequences than observed in the HIE. In a study by [Dana] Goldman et al. on the effects of cost sharing on the use of prescription drugs, drug use decreased but not indiscriminately; people with chronic conditions were less likely to reduce their disease-specific drug use than other drugs (although the extent of this varied by condition).

Some have expressed concern that consumers in high deductible plans may skimp on preventive care, although to prevent this problem from occurring, many plans waive the deductible for preventive services (i.e., the legislation authorizing HSAs permits the deductible to be waived for preventive care and periodic evaluations). However, the effects on preventive care are likely more complicated as some preventive services are provided or ordered during a non-preventive care visit; a high deductible may thus indirectly lead to a reduction in such services. And it might vary by the cost of the preventive care service—flu shots vs. colonoscopy. . . .

Enrollees in CDHP plans [may] differ from those opting for the traditional plans [so that] only high-income, healthy people will choose the CDHP option.

What Are the Trends in the Use of Personal Health Accounts Paired with High Deductible Plans?

Insurer interest in HSAs and HRAs is widespread and growing. Today, at least 75 insurers offer account-compatible plans nationwide. With the introduction of HSAs, employer interest is shifting away from HRAs to HSAs; however, because unused account balances revert to employers when an employee leaves, employer-funded HRAs are less costly to employers than equally funded HSAs—so employers are unlikely to completely shift to HSAs. A recent survey by Watson Wyatt and the National Business Group on Health found that *8% of large employers* currently offer some form of HSA and that the number is expected to increase to 26% next year. There is emerging evidence that the newest HSA products may initially be more popular among small business and individuals than larger groups; some smaller businesses that might not otherwise offer health insurance see them as a way to provide low cost coverage. A survey of America's Health Insurance Plans (AHIP) members found that 16% of small group HSA policies were sold to businesses that previously did not offer insurance. . . .

What Do We Know About Selection Effects into CDHPs?

There is concern that enrollees in CDHP plans will differ from those opting for the traditional plans, namely that only high-income, healthy people will choose the CDHP option, leaving sicker people in the traditional plans. This might increase the cost of traditional plans as there will be fewer people across whom to spread the high cost of caring for sick people. While high deductible plans coupled with accounts should attract enrollees who expect to have low medical expenses, enrollees with large expected expenses can reduce their effective out-of-pocket maximum with an account because the payments are made in dollars that one does not pay taxes on. Neither the contributions to nor the distributions from HSAs are taxed—and thus are likely to appeal to high-income employees who will view them as investment tools. . . .

Do CDHPs Reduce Patient Spending on Health Care?

Is there evidence that personal account-based plans reduce spending? Emerging reports suggest a cautious "yes." One health plan reported a reduction in facility-based services and increased reliance on generic drugs, and lower cost increases for the CDHP enrollees as compared to PPO enrollees. Parente et al. found that CDHP enrollees at one large employer had lower total expenditures than PPO enrollees and lower pharmaceutical costs, however expenditures were higher than for HMO enrollees and increased more rapidly than other groups. One employer reported a reduction of 18.7% in total medical cost after completely replacing its traditional plan with a high deductible—HRA plan.

A Qualifier

All of the findings I've noted above should be treated with caution. More work needs to be done to examine the effects before researchers and policy makers can speak confidently about the savings associated with the various CDHP products. Furthermore, how the effects of the new designs vary over time is needed to understand the implications for cost containment over time. Are these one-time reductions in use or also reductions in cost growth? At this stage it's too early to tell and we lack information to answer this question. We also lack sufficient experience with these plans to assess the impact of these plans on quality and health—and it may take longer for measurable changes in health outcomes to occur....

CDHPs Increase Needs for Information and Support of Decisions

CDHPs increase the need for information and decision support as consumers are asked to weigh trade-offs in selecting providers or treatment options—decisions that have both financial and health implications. Various tools and information are being made available in varying degrees by health plans to support more activated consumers, such as health promotion/education, risk reduction programs, consumer, decision support (e.g., comparative provider performance information, self-care and shared decision making information), disease management, directories of providers and pharmacies, information on insurance benefits and claims history, and on-line personal health information. The limited evidence to date shows that plans vary significantly in the extent to which they provide decision support. At this stage, the provision of consumer decision support remains quite limited, in scope and there is variability in the usability of the information provided.

We know little about the structure or the content of the information given to consumers in CDHPs, and . . . how they are using that information . . .

Consumers, while still largely reliant on friends, family, or a referring physician to help guide them in making choices, are increasingly reporting they have seen or used information on health care quality to make decisions. A Kaiser Family Foundation—AHRQ [Agency for Healthcare Research and Quality, a federal agency]—Harvard sponsored national survey of consumers conducted in 2004 showed that 35% of consumers have seen information comparing the quality of plans and providers, and about half of those who had seen it reported they had used this information to make a decision about their care. Yet empirical studies conducted in the past 5–7 years find that most consumers are not using these tools to make decisions, and that frequently consumers could not easily or correctly evaluate the content of the material. Studies also find a strong correlation between education and use of the Internet for health information; thus, the utility of decision tools may vary substantially among different subpopulations.

Various problems exist today in the provision of consumer information. First there is limited information collected and publicly available. Second, there is a lack of standardization in measurement and reporting to enable consumers to compare performance across providers and treatments. Third, the information currently provided to consumers typically is not easily evaluable and consequently may be confusing or create the potential for the consumer to make the wrong choice. Presentation format and design is critical in influencing how people weigh their decision choices and in whether they attend to and comprehend the information. The evaluability of the information becomes critically important because there is more at stake, the choices are more complex, and the volume of information is likely to be greater—all of which may overwhelm the consumer. . . .

Currently, we know little about the structure or the content of the information given to consumers in CDHPs, and whether and how they are using that information in their decision-making. Future research should explore the extent to which information tools are made available, whether existing tools provided in CDHPs have the characteristics noted above, whether the information is evaluable, and how this information is actually used by consumers in CDHP models. There also continues to be limited collection and transparency of performance information at all levels of the health system, and in particular for those areas, providers, and treatments that are most critical to facilitating informed consumer decision-making.

Market Models Do Not Apply to America's Current Health Care Crisis

David R. Francis

About the author: *David R. Francis is a journalist with the daily newspaper* Christian Science Monitor.

The United States faces a medical emergency. Costs of the nation's healthcare system are growing so fast they are out of control. Many employers are dumping escalating healthcare expenses for both employees and their retired workers as fast as they can manage, fearing a loss of competitiveness.

So far, the White House and other would-be physicians have decided that the answer is more of the same—the magic of consumer choice in a free market. But some are skeptical that this will provide a real cure.

The Flaws in Market-Based Health Care

"The whole idea is unsound," says Arnold Relman, a Harvard Medical School expert. Yet influential people in Washington have persuaded themselves that a more competitive healthcare system will slash costs enough to keep it workable.

The numbers seem to back up Dr. Relman's conclusion.

Currently, the average American consumes $6,420 worth of healthcare services a year. That's more than $12,200 a year for the average family. It's the most inefficient medical system among industrial nations.

US healthcare costs have reached $1.6 trillion a year. That's 15 percent of the nation's economy, up from 5 percent in

1963. Other industrial nations devote less than 10 percent of gross domestic product to healthcare.

The [United States] will need to debate and consider implementing a changed system, probably a form of a "single-payer system."

The US pays more than twice as much per person as other wealthy countries. "Yet it has little if anything to show in terms of outcomes," notes Dean Baker, an economist with the Center for Economic and Policy Research, in a new study.

Moreover, costs are rising at a rate of 7 to 9 percent a year. That's not sustainable, notes Relman. "We are not getting anywhere near our money's worth."

US life expectancies are shorter, infant mortality rates higher, and other health measures are worse than in nearly all other wealthy nations.

Approximately 45 million Americans lack health insurance all year; about 80 million go without it for part of the year.

A Crisis in Health Care Could Bring Needed Changes

In the long run, such a consumer-driven medical system is not likely to be politically viable. It may take five to 10 years, but at some point the tide of political and public opinion will turn. Then the US will need to debate and consider implementing a changed system, probably a form of a "single-payer" system that would be less expensive and provide quality healthcare.

"Something will happen at some point because we can't afford [today's system]," says Mr. Baker. "But everyone is trying to do their best to will it away. Politicians are scared to death to talk about this. You can't even get a serious discussion."

Rep. Dennis Kucinich of Ohio proposed a universal health-care plan in his unsuccessful bid for the [2004] Democratic presidential nomination. It got little attention. The single-payer system would have saved $286 billion a year on paper-work alone, his experts held.

Medical Care Is Not a Market Commodity

The root of the problem, Relman holds, is that medical care is not really a "market" in the classical economic sense. Health problems are often complex. Patients rely on professional expertise rather than their own consumer judgment. So trying to treat healthcare as a conventional market is bound to fail.

Nevertheless, medical care has taken on the trappings of the market over the past four decades, Relman argues. Instead of a system of mostly personal transactions between physicians and patients 'that took place in patients' homes, doctors' offices, and not-for-profit hospitals and clinics, it has now become a "new medical-industrial complex," he [wrote] in a March [2005] issue of *New Republic*. He sees this industrial transformation undermining the professional values of physicians, "which are surely an essential ingredient of any decent medical care system. . . . Financial incentives were replacing the service ethic of doctors and hospitals as the providers of care began to compete for market share and larger income."

Market Approaches Fail to Contain Costs

Many conservative business and health-policy experts continue holding unshakable faith in a market solution to rising costs. That view emerged in the creation of tax-deductible "health savings accounts" in the 2003 [congressional] bill providing prescription-drug coverage to seniors [in 2006]. The idea [was] that medical ads should be encouraged to help consumers evaluate medical goods and services and thus use their account funds more wisely.

But costs are still going up. Drug inflation is so high, seniors [paid] more for drugs [in 2006] on average than they did in 2000, even after they [got] the new government subsidy.

Leaving Medicaid to the Market Has Destroyed the Program in Tennessee

Trudy Lieberman

About the author: *Trudy Lieberman is the health policy editor of* Consumer Reports, *a nonpartisan consumers' advocacy magazine and research group.*

Every day this summer [2005] a couple of dozen folks staged a sit-in outside the office of Tennessee's Democratic governor, Phil Bredesen, to protest drastic cuts in TennCare, the state's Medicaid program. The protest was "the best thing I've put effort into in my life," says TennCare enrollee Glen Barnhill, a 45-year-old from Nashville who stocked grocery shelves at Kroger before he was rendered a quadriplegic from a gunshot wound to his brain. "If we don't keep fighting," Barnhill says between puffs on his ventilator, "these people are going to die."

TennCare, a Once-Model Medicaid System

Nearly 200,000 Tennesseans lost their health insurance in July [2005], while 379,000 others now have limited prescription drug coverage and face more benefit cuts this winter. Until this summer, these mostly poor residents had comprehensive health coverage under the boldest, most visionary expansion of Medicaid the United States had ever seen. TennCare covered two groups that have trouble buying insurance in every state: low-income adults whose employers do not provide medical benefits, and people with health conditions that make them uninsurable. At its peak, TennCare covered almost 1.4 million people. By the late 1990s, only 14 percent of the state's population was uninsured—while in states like California and Texas, one-quarter of the population had no insurance.

At its conception in 1994, TennCare looked like a national model for expanding Medicaid coverage [for the poor].

Today TennCare is $60 million in the red, and Tennessee is just another state struggling to keep poor and terminally ill people insured. All across the country, Medicaid offices are reducing benefits, freezing provider payments and kicking people off the rolls. But the outcry has been loudest in Tennessee—both because its program was once the best and because no other state has slashed Medicaid so deeply. Governor Bredesen, who made his fortune in managed care, has refused to meet with the protesters in public, as they've requested. He has also ignored calls for a special legislative session to reconsider the TennCare cutbacks. The state's senior senator, Republican majority leader Bill Frist, has not been helpful either. Before he was elected to the Senate, Frist championed TennCare; now he says the program's troubles are a state matter, and he can't get involved. "It's ironic how Senator Frist stands up for Terri Schiavo [a Florida woman disabled by a severe stroke; a battle took place for over a decade over her husband's petition to courts to let her die]," says protest organizer Lori Smith, "yet denies medical care to his own people in Tennessee."

The ironies don't stop there. At its conception in 1994, TennCare looked like a national model for expanding Medicaid coverage. Born in the days of [President] Lyndon Johnson's Great Society [domestic social programs proposed or enacted during President Johnson's years in office (1963–1969)] as a way of covering the poor, Medicaid has evolved into the nation's largest health insurance plan, now covering 53 million Americans. The federal government matches the money a state puts up for the program, but states have broad latitude to add benefits and enroll more residents as they see fit. As President [Bill] Clinton's plan for national healthcare collapsed and the number of uninsured continued to mount in the mid 1990s, Tennessee leaders came up with a creative solution: Redirect money that hospitals were already spending on care for the uninsured into a unified program that would cover more people and better control costs.

Crafted at a time when policy experts believed managed care was the antidote to rising medical costs, TennCare relied on HMOs [Health Maintenance Organizations] to provide benefits. The theory was that if the state did managed care right, it could cover a good chunk of the uninsured. But TennCare's HMOs did little managing. First Health Services Corporation, owned by a company that Bredesen founded, failed to implement federal requirements designed to insure that drugs are prescribed properly—but never lost its contract with the state. The state allowed two HMOs to "cover" residents even though they were undercapitalized and could not pay providers for care their patients received. Eventually the state assumed the risk and responsibility for all patients' medical expenses. But Tennessee continued to pay the managed care companies handsome fees—simply for processing claims. For the HMOs it was a sweet deal: fees but no risk.

Dismantling TennCare

Former Governor Don Sundquist, a Republican, sped along TennCare's slide into insolvency. In 2002, during routine Medicaid renegotiations with the federal government, Sundquist agreed to give back some federal matching funds—even though the program was already running into financial trouble and starting to trim residents from its rolls. Until 2002 anyone who was uninsurable could join TennCare, regardless of income, in return for paying premiums; those with higher incomes paid more. That changed dramatically in 2002, when the state closed TennCare to anyone with an income above poverty level—and stopped enrolling people who could not buy insurance because of bad health.

That same year, Tennessee voters rejected an income tax that could have helped pay for TennCare. The governor has refused to support subsequent proposals for new sales taxes on alcohol and tobacco. "There's no political appetite in his state for new taxes," says TennCare spokesperson Michael Drescher.

Patients Cope with TennCare's Decline

If Tennessee can't, or won't, pay for medical care, it's fair to ask a stark question: How can the thousands of people thrown off the rolls—including heart-transplant patients and people with lupus, diabetes and severe mental illness—survive?

Kathy Chamberlain would like to know. The 46-year-old, who used to play acoustic guitar at Nashville blues cafes, fights back tears as she describes an incessant ringing in her ears, the result of slipping on a puddle of water in a local supermarket and hitting her head on the floor. She has never been the same since, and she relied on TennCare to pay for her treatment and for antidepressants—drugs she didn't need before the accident. Those drugs now cost $639 a month; a discount card from the state, sent to TennCare enrollees who lost their coverage, pares her bill to $463. Chamberlain still can't afford it; she has to use her mother's credit card to buy her prescriptions.

"I have never encountered anything that I could not change until this," Chamberlain says. Even if she could afford to buy insurance, her illness would prevent her from getting a policy. She can't change that, either.

The thousands of Chamberlain's fellow Tennesseans who have been kicked off TennCare haven't seen the worst of it yet. The Center on Budget and Policy Priorities estimates that the massive loss of TennCare coverage will lead to an increase in uncompensated care that will cost "safety net" hospitals and clinics in Tennessee as much as $450 million annually. Waiting lists will grow longer, and the lost revenue could force some hospitals and clinics to close. Mary Bufwack, director of Nashville's United Neighborhood Health Services [UNHS], says her budget is not big enough to serve all the newly uninsured who are showing up at her five clinics for the indigent. Forty percent of UNHS's budget had been coming from TennCare payments.

Estimates [suggest] that TennCare cuts will result in the deaths of as many as 3,311 people over the next fifteen years.

Some former TennCare patients are turning to drug-company assistance programs for help, but the wait for free drugs is six to eight weeks—if their incomes are low enough to make them eligible. Others are begging doctors for medication samples left by sales representatives. Hickman County healthcare activist Cindy Clark says doctors are running out of free samples. "They are overwhelmed," says Clark. "We see a disaster taking place in this state."

A disaster indeed. The Center for Health Services Research at the University of Tennessee-Memphis estimates that TennCare cuts will result in the deaths of as many as 3,311 people over the next fifteen years. Fifty-two-year-old Diane Wood can only hope she's not one of the casualties. Wood, who lives in the rolling hills east of Nashville, calls herself "fortunate" to have breast cancer; so far, women with breast or cervical cancer have been allowed to stay on TennCare. [2005's] remake of TennCare instituted severe caps on prescription drugs, limiting recipients to two brand-name prescriptions and three generics per month. That has forced Wood to choose which of her other illnesses—diabetes, osteoporosis, failing kidneys—she will treat. Wood, who earns $50 a week baby-sitting her grandchildren, has decided to treat her cancer and kidney disease and say "to heck with" the diabetes and osteoporosis.

"Caps are the crudest cost-containment policy I can ever imagine," says Dr. Stephen Soumerai, a professor and drug-policy researcher at Harvard University Medical School. "What caps do is completely counter to everything we know based on research in the field." They certainly don't save money in the long run. When people like Wood can't get the medicines they need, they get sicker and end up in nursing homes and other institutions where the cost of care is greater than the savings generated by the caps.

The Role of Physicians

A growing number of Tennessee doctors, particularly specialists and those in rural areas, refuse to take TennCare patients. Doctors grumbled from the start that the state paid them too little to treat these patients. Like doctors everywhere, they prefer to serve those insured by commercial carriers like Aetna or Blue Cross, which pay more than Medicaid. In a recent survey of its members, the Tennessee Medical Association found that although 88 percent said they still work with TennCare, 20 percent are not taking new TennCare patients and 27 percent are considering ending their contract with the program. The main reason, says association senior vice president Russell Miller, is that cuts in benefits are compromising the care doctors want to give—and increasing the legal liability they are exposed to.

[In 2005] legislators axed 104,213 people from Missouri Medicaid—and ordered the state to get out of the Medicaid business altogether by 2008.

Doctors who still accept TennCare patients know what's going to happen. "We kept a lot of people from dying for over a decade," Nashville gastroenterologist Robert Herring said recently, after a long day of performing colonoscopies on people about to lose their coverage. "It's a shame we couldn't provide a bridge until we have national health insurance," the doctor said. "Now I am going to cry."

Medicaid Is in Crisis Nationwide

Outside of Tennessee, the most radical response to the nationwide Medicaid crisis has unfolded in Missouri. [In 2005] legislators axed 104,213 people from Missouri Medicaid—and ordered the state to get out of the Medicaid business altogether by 2008. Where Missouri was once one of the dozen states with the lowest number of uninsured residents, it will become one of the dozen with the highest number after all its cuts take effect. Already, the state has stopped paying for feeding tubes and nutritional formula for thousands of residents with brain damage and other disabilities. It won't pay for other lifesaving items, like breathing machines, either.

Tennessee once aspired to [lead] in expanding health coverage. Its current governor wants to make it the . . . model for retrenching and privatizing Medicaid.

In October [2005], the federal government gave Florida permission to radically transform its Medicaid program into a "defined contribution" arrangement instead of an entitlement. Recipients will get a set amount of money for medical care, and private insurers will make many of the decisions about coverage—with no public scrutiny. If Florida's plan becomes the model for other states, as some healthcare activists fear, it will mean that poor people will get less and less medical care over time.

While the states chop benefits, the federal government is also aiming to cut its share of Medicaid funding. Congress has ordered a commission—chaired, by former Tennessee Governor Sundquist—to recommend ways to slash $10 billion from the federal government's Medicaid budget. While the cuts will devastate thousands of Americans, they will do little to address the real financial problem facing the US healthcare system: how to create a new revenue source that will provide coverage for everyone and spread the risk of illness, much the way Social Security spreads the risk of citizens having no income in old age.

Attempts to Fully Privatize Medicaid

While Tennessee once aspired to be a leader in expanding health coverage, its current governor wants to make it the national model for retrenching and privatizing Medicaid. A confidential document called "Back to Medicaid Kick-off," prepared by TennCare's deputy commissioner and the state commissioner of finance and administration, not only outlines steps for gutting TennCare but also vows to "set the stage to allow the Governor a broader healthcare reform platform." In the view of Michele Johnson, a lawyer with the Tennessee Justice Center, Bredesen's "political future depends on transforming Medicaid into a market-based system, and he believes he can ride the market-based approach to the national stage."

Protesters at the state capitol ... rang [a bell] to represent every Tennessean affected by ... TennCare cuts. It took four days ...

Bob Corney, the governor's communications director, says the governor has no plans to run for any office except his current one; Bredesen will seek re-election next year. But the governor's stand on Medicaid has already brought him national attention. At a University of North Carolina "emerging issues" forum in February, and again in June at the National Press Club in Washington, Bredesen gave his vision for what he called Medicaid 2.0. The governor called for all Medicaid recipients to pay "something"—i.e., higher deductibles and co-payments. Medicaid, Bredesen declared, should pay only for treatments that work and for "things that are important."

While few experts would quarrel with paying only for "what works," it's far easier said than done. No drug company or medical-technology firm peddling ineffective treatments will give up its business without a political fight. And shifting costs to those who can't pay for treatment only increases long-term costs to the state.

Bredesen has steadfastly refused to seek new money to insure those who are being booted off TennCare. Indeed, his staff's "Back to Medicaid Kick-off" document sets a goal of stifling any alternative proposals for new revenue. Bredesen has also declined to dip into the state's $200 million surplus funds. "You can't revenue your way out of this problem," insists TennCare spokesperson Drescher.

Prospects for TennCare Look Bleak

However noble the TennCare experiment was, it ultimately demonstrated the futility of states' efforts to solve a national problem by themselves. In late July [2005] protesters at the state capitol hauled a bell from the Edgehill United Methodist Church onto Nashville's legislative plaza. They rang it to represent every Tennessean affected by the TennCare cuts. It took four days to complete the roll call.

The tolling of that bell is the real lesson of TennCare for people all across America: The bell tolls for thee.

CHAPTER 4

How Should America's Healthcare System Be Transformed?

Chapter Preface

Possibly the only point of agreement among policy makers, politicians, and health-care advocates is that something in our present system must change. The values underlying their calls for change are very different, however, depending on whether the argument is being made by conservatives or libertarians, on the one hand, or liberals and progressives, on the other.

Health-care advocates to the right of center tend to emphasize individualism as the answer to America's current health-care crisis: smart consumerism, individual responsibility, and the right to exercise as much individual freedom as possible in making health-care decisions. From congressional hearings to books to talk shows to op-ed pieces in daily newspapers, conservatives and libertarians have emphasized the role of informed choice in using health care frugally. Members of President George W. Bush's administration have claimed that responsibility for the high cost of health care rests with individual policy holders, who "consume [health care] as if it were free." Tell "consumers" what the actual price of medical services is and create health-insurance plans that provide incentives to reduce usage of services through high deductibles, these thinkers claim, and individuals will become savvier (and less frequent) consumers of health care. Similarly, these critics believe that high-deductible policies, besides lowering premium costs, will also reward responsible behavior: individuals who do not smoke, who are not overweight, who exercise and eat well, are likely to have fewer out-of-pocket (nondeductible) expenses and to pay lower premiums than individuals who do not take care of themselves. Moreover, they point out that health-care reforms that stress individual decision making would give consumers more control over what providers and institutions to support—for example, an individual could choose not to use the services of a physician who performed abortions or a hospital whose practices he or she did not approve of.

Liberal and progressive reformers generally view health care as a collective responsibility that a civil society should provide for all of its members. They view the right's current emphasis on personal responsibility as little more than a rationale for further privatizing health care and shifting responsibility from government and employers to individual workers. In their various proposals for transforming American health care, liberals and progressives emphasize collective rather than personal responsibility: extending the federal Medicare program to all citizens; allowing all Americans to join the same government-funded and -administered health plan that members of congress enjoy; making the same level of government-funded care available to all citizens.

Arguments between those wishing to minimize government involvement in individual lives and those believing that government should act as a force for the collective good have been a part of America's social and political landscape since the country's earliest days. These arguments have grown more acute over time; America has shifted from a society that acknowledged acting for the common good as a widely embraced civic virtue to one in which individual desires and beliefs have become preeminent. With the decline in labor unions and television broadcasting and the rise of highly stratified markets and solitary pursuits like Web surfing and iPod listening, contemporary Americans now seem more invested in individual than in collective pursuits. The motto on U.S. currency, *E pluribus unum*—out of many, the one—seems increasingly to be reversing itself: out of the one, the many.

Government's Involvement in Health Care Should Reward Individual Responsibility

Michael F. Cannon

About the author: *Michael F. Cannon is the director of Health Policy Studies at the Cato Institute, a conservative/libertarian think tank.*

The last thing patients need is for the government to inject more socialism into their health care in the name of expanding coverage. To borrow a phrase from President [Ronald] Reagan, government is not the solution to U.S. health care problems. It is the problem.

Most of America's health care is private, so many assume it operates as a free market. In truth, it is dominated by the government, resulting in high costs and stifling bureaucracy.

The federal government effectively socializes 86% of all health spending, a greater share than in 17 other industrialized countries, including Canada (though other features make these systems less free).

Government Health Care Discourages Individual Responsibility

By discouraging individual responsibility, the government guarantees irresponsibility. We pay less attention to our health and demand more care—with little regard to the costs we impose on others or the rising prices that result. (Should it surprise us that health insurance is unaffordable for millions?) Those footing the bill—employers, insurers and the government—try to impose responsibility in ways both offensive and harmful (read: managed care).

Estimates by Harvard economist Martin Feldstein suggest that the federal government's quasi-socialization of private insurance alone will leave us nearly $200 billion worse off this year. Moreover, Chris Conover of Duke University estimates that health regulations will leave us $128 billion worse off. Taken together, that is more than what taxpayers will spend on Medicare or Medicaid in 2004. The only way to make health care affordable is to get the government out.

Health savings accounts restore individual responsibility, curb medical inflation and will make health care and insurance more affordable for millions.

[2004] Democratic presidential hopeful John Kerry [saw] only bad outcomes—rising prices, millions of uninsured—rather than root causes. He therefore recommend[ed] more socialism (under the guise of "expanding coverage") even though this would further increase costs and make a total government takeover inevitable.

Though President [George W.] Bush's record is far from perfect, he supports strengthening health savings accounts, which reduce the government's role in health care. Health savings accounts restore individual responsibility, curb medical inflation and will make health care and insurance more affordable for millions.

Ronald Reagan demonstrated that free markets are superior to socialism.

So why do we continue to tolerate socialism in our health care system?

True Health-Care Reform Must Return Decision-Making to Individuals

Robert E. Moffit, Grace V. Smith, and Jennifer A. Marshall

About the authors: *Robert E. Moffit is director of the Center for Health Policy Studies at The Heritage Foundation, a conservative think tank in Washington, DC. Grace V. Smith is research assistant in Domestic Policy Studies at The Heritage Foundation. Jennifer A. Marshall is director of Domestic Policy Studies at The Heritage Foundation.*

A mericans are deeply concerned about health care. By nearly all accounts, rising health care costs are contributing to their anxiety about health care financing, while complex and impersonal administrative systems leave many feeling personally disenfranchised when it comes to making key health care decisions. The current system of third-party payment, which governs government- and employment-based insurance arrangements, undermines personal decision-making in health care while increasing the difficulty of individuals and families in coping with employment decisions and the transitions that accompany changes in life. Meanwhile, technological and biomedical advances present troubling ethical implications for millions of individuals and families.

These various problems are interrelated and require systemic solutions. Reforming health care is about more than reducing costs and expanding individual coverage, important as those are. A primary goal of reform should be the achievement of compatibility between individuals' personal values and their health care choices. Healthcare reform should create a real free market in which Americans are free to choose health coverage that is consistent with their ethical, moral, and religious convictions.

Personal Freedom: Conscience and Dollars

Freedom of conscience ought to include the freedom to choose health care coverage that reflects one's ethical or moral values, physicians who respect one's values, and courses of medical treatment that embody those values. But while legislatures and courts debate such controversial issues as the use of embryonic stem cell research and physician-assisted suicide, individuals and families remain almost powerless to spend their own money on health plans that respect their most deeply held beliefs.

Most Americans are on the receiving end of third-party payment decisions and do not directly control the dollars that finance health benefits and medical treatment. If, for example, a person believes in the sanctity of human life from conception to natural death, he may still be required to finance benefits and medical practices he considers morally wrong through health insurance premiums. In fact, many states mandate that insurance companies provide benefits that include controversial treatments, such as in-vitro fertilization, sterilization, and contraception.

Individuals and families should be free to make their own decisions and exercise their own conscience in . . . sensitive matters [of biomedical ethics].

Every year, Americans pay hundreds of billions of dollars in premiums to health insurance plans over which they have often little to no personal control. Most Americans today receive healthcare coverage through either private insurance, usually purchased by their employer, or government programs, such as Medicare and Medicaid. In both cases, the person is not the primary decision-maker when it comes to benefits. Instead, insurance executives, managed care networks, employers, and government officials choose the health plans that will be available and what benefits they will include. In fact, most Americans do not have a personal choice of health plans, and the choices they do have are often superficial, with different plans having the same delivery networks. This must change.

The Biomedical Revolution: The Promise and the Peril

As medical researchers explore new biotechnologies in search for path-breaking treatments for ailments and diseases, they are redefining medicine. Tomorrow's doctors will have far greater means at their disposal to improve and extend the quality of human life than doctors do today.

Progress and promises are not without complication and moral dilemma, however. The hot-button issues at the intersection of health, technology, public policy, medical ethics, and individual morality will multiply. Currently, controversial practices such as abortion and emergency contraception divide the American public, even as new ethical challenges are developing. In laboratories across the globe, researchers harvest stem cells from human embryos, and tomorrow human cloning will no longer be the province of science fiction thrillers. With advances in biotechnology, nanotechnology, and genetic engineering, Americans will face challenges that even policymakers have not even begun to imagine. While the general public wrestles with the moral implications of these new developments, they are routinely translated into new medical treatments and procedures—and sooner or later covered as benefits under health insurance policies. While these issues are debated in the public square, individuals and families should be free to make their own decisions and exercise their own conscience in these sensitive matters.

Toward Greater Personal Freedom

Congress can take two important steps to promote greater personal freedom in healthcare:

- *Liberalize the tax treatment of health insurance for individuals and families.* Hundreds of billions of dollars in federal and state tax breaks for health insurance largely favor employment-based plans. The current bias in the tax treatment of healthcare means that workers who purchase health insurance through their employers enjoy an unlimited tax break for that coverage, while workers who purchase an individual or group plan on the open market have to do so with after-tax dollars. For many middle class families, this inequity in the tax treatment of health insurance makes the purchase of a personal health plan prohibitively expensive. To rectify this unequal treatment in the federal tax code, Congress should, at the very least, provide the same tax breaks to those who choose to purchase health plans from sources other than their employers, such as unions, fraternal organizations, and faith-based associations.

- *Open access to new health plans through interstate commerce in health insurance.* Unlike many goods and services sold in the United States, health insurance is mostly regulated at the state level, and different states' plans are subject to different rules and benefit mandates. Practically speaking, families' health plan choices are often limited to those available in the states in which they reside. Opening the health insurance market to interstate commerce and creating regional or national markets in which families could choose from a wide variety of health plans—including values-driven plans—would increase consumer freedom and empower individuals and families to enroll in health plans that fit their needs and values. Creating a national market for health insurance would also reduce family costs because insurance providers would face broader and more intense competition. Rep. John Shadegg (R-AZ) and Sen. Jim DeMint (R-SC) have introduced legislation, The Health Care Choice Act, to expand family choices and bring down health insurance costs.

Health-care reform should give individuals and families the freedom to make values-driven decisions about their care. Personal decisions about health and medical treatment touch the core of our beliefs about life, death, and morality. Individuals are far better equipped than government officials and private employers to make decisions that reflect their consciences. Values-driven health-care reform would empower individuals to make such decisions, by putting them—rather than government or corporate officials—in control of their health care.

Health Care Should Be a Personal Responsibility

Radley Balko

About the author: *Radley Balko is a policy analyst with the conservative/libertarian Cato Institute.*

This June [2004] *Time* magazine and ABC News will host a three-day summit on obesity. [Former] ABC News anchor Peter Jennings, who last December anchored the prime time special "How to Get Fat Without Really Trying," will host. Judging by the scheduled program, the summit promises to be a pep rally for media, nutrition activists, and policy makers— all agitating for a panoply of government anti-obesity initiatives, including prohibiting junk food in school vending machines, federal funding for new bike trails and sidewalks, more demanding labels on foodstuffs, restrictive food marketing to children, and prodding the food industry into more "responsible" behavior. In other words, bringing government between you and your waistline.

Politicians have already climbed aboard. President [George W.] Bush earmarked $200 million in his budget for anti-obesity measures. State legislatures and school boards across the country have begun banning snacks and soda from school campuses and vending machines. Sen. Joe Lieberman and Oakland [California] Mayor Jerry Brown, among others, have called for a "fat tax" on high-calorie foods. Congress is now considering menu-labeling legislation, which would force restaurants to send every menu item to the laboratory for nutritional testing.

Radley Balko, "Beyond Personal Responsibility," Techcentralstation.com, May 17, 2004. Reproduced by permission.

Personal Responsibility Is at the Root of Health

This is the wrong way to fight obesity. Instead of manipulating or intervening in the array of food options available to American consumers, our government ought to be working to foster a sense of responsibility in and ownership of our own health and well-being. But we're doing just the opposite.

For decades now, America's health care system has been migrating toward socialism. Your well-being, shape, and condition have increasingly been deemed matters of "public health," instead of matters of personal responsibility. Our lawmakers just enacted a huge entitlement that requires some people to pay for other people's medicine. Sen. Hillary Clinton just penned a lengthy article in the *New York Times Magazine* calling for yet more federal control of health care. All of the Democrat candidates for president boasted plans to push health care further into the public sector. More and more, states are preventing private health insurers from charging overweight and obese clients higher premiums, which effectively removes any financial incentive for maintaining a healthy lifestyle.

We're becoming less responsible for our own health, and more responsible for everyone else's. Your heart attack drives up the cost of my premiums and office visits. And if the government is paying for my anti-cholesterol medication, what incentive is there for me to put down the cheeseburger?

Collective Responsibility Restricts Individual Freedom

This collective ownership of private health then paves the way for even more federal restrictions on consumer choice and civil liberties. A society where everyone is responsible for everyone else's well-being is a society more apt to accept government restrictions, for example—on what McDonalds can put on its menu, what Safeway or Kroger can put on grocery shelves, or holding food companies responsible for the bad habits of unhealthy consumers.

A growing army of nutritionist activists and food industry foes are egging the process on. Margo Wootan of the Center for Science in the Public Interest has said, "We've got to move beyond 'personal responsibility.'" The largest organization of trial lawyers now encourages its members to weed jury pools of candidates who show "personal responsibility bias." The title of Jennings' special from last December—"How to Get Fat Without Really Trying"—reveals his intent, which is to relieve viewers of responsibility for their own condition. Indeed, Jennings ended the program with an impassioned plea for government intervention to fight obesity.

The best way to alleviate the obesity "public health" crisis is to remove obesity from the realm of public health. It doesn't belong there. It's difficult to think of anything more private and of less public concern than what we choose to put into our bodies. It only becomes a public matter when we force the public to pay for the consequences of those choices. If policymakers want to fight obesity, they'll halt the creeping socialization of medicine, and move to return individual Americans' ownership of their own health and well-being back to individual Americans.

Accountability Demands Individual Responsibility

That means freeing insurance companies to reward healthy lifestyles, and penalize poor ones. It means halting plans to further socialize medicine and health care. Congress should also increase access to medical and health savings accounts, which give consumers the option of rolling money reserved for health care into a retirement account. These accounts introduce accountability into the health care system, and encourage caution with one's health care dollar. When money we spend on health care doesn't belong to our employer or the government, but is money we could devote to our own retirement, we're less likely to run to the doctor at the first sign of a cold.

We'll all make better choices about diet, exercise, and personal health when someone else isn't paying for the consequences of those choices.

Health Insurance and "Personal Responsibility": Shifting the Bill from the Employer to the Worker

Judi King

About the author: *Judi King is the director of the University of Alabama-Birmingham Center for Labor Education and Research and an associate professor in the UAB School of Business.*

The lead story in the February 1, 2005 *Birmingham [Alabama] News* stopped a lot of us in our tracks. "Shifting health care's bill," the headline proclaimed. "Employer-provided medical insurance would end under plans of Bush, GOP."

A trend that began in 2004 has apparently picked up steam, with supporters in business and Congress anxious to move the concept of "personal responsibility" to a family's health care. As consumers of health care in this "ownership society," you and your family will ultimately bear the financial burden of your health choices. Make good choices, the theory suggests, and you will save money; make poor choices and you will pay. Not a bad theory—until you or a loved one gets sick.

Skyrocketing Health Care Costs

Anyone who has negotiated a labor agreement in the past 20 years has had to contend with the enormous increases in health insurance costs. Every penny we gained in wage increases—and then some—went to defray increases in health insurance. Double digit increases year after year left workers with smaller paychecks and less generous health benefits. Employers, meanwhile, could do little to stem the increases. Those paying health benefits for retirees, especially, sought to reduce or eliminate those benefits in the face of ever-increasing costs.

Unlike countries with national health care plans, the United States has developed over the past 60 years a system of employer-based health insurance. Most workers obtained their insurance from the group plans provided at the workplace. In a few cases—mostly unionized employers—the employer paid the total premium for this insurance; in most cases the employee shared in that cost. As the costs have risen, more and more employers have expressed a desire to get out of the health insurance business entirely.

Whose Responsibility?

If employers no longer want to provide health insurance, then who should undertake that responsibility? Any discussion that tends toward societal or governmental responsibility sends policy makers and politicians scurrying for cover. That leaves the individual—the party least equipped to pay the freight—to take on that challenge. And here's where "personal responsibility" and "ownership" come in.

"Personal responsibility" ... [meansl if you have to pay a larger portion of your health care costs, you won't make frivolous trips to the physician.

There has been a lot of talk over the past several years about "consumerism" in health care. This consumer focus really has two aspects:

1. If you make better health decisions—through diet, exercise, and other lifestyle choices—you will be healthier and will have fewer medical expenses.

2. The more that insurance pays toward your medical bills, the more likely you are to use medical services. This

concept, known as *moral hazard* in the insurance industry, means that you will use less medical care if you have to reach into your pocket to pay for that care.

Underlying the proposals to introduce "personal responsibility" into health care, then, is the belief that, if you have to pay a larger portion of your health care costs, you won't make frivolous trips to the physician and hospital, and you won't demand all those unnecessary tests. Furthermore, you'll make better health choices when you realize that you'll have to pay more of the cost of your health care. Merely getting sick or dying, apparently, is not incentive enough.

Enter the Health Savings Account

For many years workers have had the opportunity to set aside pre-tax dollars in a Flexible Spending Account (FSA). FSAs are used for dependent care and medical expenses. The major drawback is that all the money set aside must be used within the calendar year; any money not claimed is lost. Many workers have shied away from FSAs because they have been wary of the "use it or lose it" provision.

In January, 2004, the tax code began to allow a new pre-tax savings device: the Health Savings Account (HSA). These new accounts have many advantages:

1. the employer can also contribute;
2. the balance of the account can roll over from year to year;
3. the HSA is portable and can move with the employee if he or she changes jobs;
4. HSAs can earn interest, and
5. qualified withdrawals from HSAs are also tax-free.

The downside? HSAs can only be offered in conjunction with high-deductible health insurance plans. The annual deductible must be at least $1000 for single coverage and $2000 for family coverage. Contributions to the HSA can equal the amount of the annual deductible, up to a cap of $2650 for individuals and $5250 for families (year 2005 limits). The deductible and contribution limits are revised annually.

High-deductible plans, of course, don't pay medical costs until the yearly deductible is met, although plans can exclude some preventive care from the deductible. The HSA is intended to cover that initial high deductible, or other medical expenses the family may incur during the year.

Are HSAs Good for You?

There is no question that an account like an HSA can provide tax benefits for many families. Health savings accounts are the only individual accounts that provide pre-tax withholding and tax-free withdrawals. If the employer contributes to the account then the worker saves even more.

Young and/or healthy workers may find HSAs attractive because they have few medical bills, and they can keep the money in the account, drawing interest, until they finally have occasion to use it. It's possible that some workers might be able to build a substantial fund to finance future medical costs.

But HSAs are not cost-free, as some might suggest. Some of the costs a worker might encounter:

- Even with a high-deductible insurance plan, the worker would still have to pay premiums. High-deductible plans tend to have lower premiums—usually 20% to 40% lower—but there is still a monthly premium to pay.

- HSA administrators charge fees to open the accounts and monthly fees to maintain them.

- The tax advantages of HSAs tend to fall to the wealthiest taxpayers. For those with low incomes, there are few if any tax benefits.

- The prospect of having to pay a huge deductible—as high as $5000 under some family plans—is daunting to most of us. If one uses an HSA to pay the deductible, then there are no funds to pay other medical expenses, such as prescriptions, dental bills, or eye care.

One recent study found that those who used health savings accounts had incomes 48% higher than those who selected low-deductible plans. A second study found that those who opted of HSAs were "significantly healthier on every dimension measured."[1] Yet another study found that 49% of those with deductibles above $500 per year—a much lower figure than what HSAs currently allow—had outstanding medical debt, compared with 32% of those with low-deductible coverage.[2]

Are HSAs Good for the Health Care System?

What difference does it make if higher-income or healthier people select these plans? Will it affect you or your employer-provided insurance?

Eventually it will, in some very dramatic ways:

1. If the healthiest people opt out of any particular insurance program, it leaves the remaining plans to pick up a disproportionate share of those who are most sick. Insurance relies on the concept of the risk pool, with each insurer spreading the risk of having very sick people in the pool over a vast group of much healthier beneficiaries. If the pool contains more and more sick people— and fewer and fewer healthy people—the insurer faces what is known as *adverse selection*. Rates must go up in the pool to cover the higher risk. So, if healthy people leave your plan to go to a high-deductible plan, your rates invariably will go up.

2. As the costs of the low-deductible plans escalate, we can expect more and more employers to offer *only* high-deductible plans.

3. Over the long term, what the Bush administration is proposing is to move health insurance from the workplace to the individual level. As more and more people sign on to these defined contribution plans, employers will ease out of the insurance business altogether. The President's current health care plan promote HSAs along with proposals to provide tax credits for purchasing *individual* insurance, changes in who can offer health insurance, and a "national marketplace" for consumers to shop across state lines to buy coverage. There is nothing in these proposals that encourages employers to continue to offer good workplace-based health insurance, but plenty to encourage workers to seek individual coverage.

4. HSAs propose to solve the ever-increasing costs of health care by making consumers responsible for their own health decisions. The largest driver of high costs, however, is the extended hospital stay after surgery. Even with high-deductible plans, the costs of those stays falls to the insurer; after a patient pays a deductible of $1500 or $2000, the balance of a $50,000 hospital bill would still be paid by the insurer. How would such a system rein in escalating health care costs?

Over the next four years, we'll be hearing more and more about being "empowered" to make our own decisions about health care and, as the Social Security debate heats up, our retirement income. Younger workers, having faced no medical bills and being unable to imagine ever getting old enough to retire, will be especially vulnerable to these enticements about "ownership" and "personal responsibility." It is our job to make sure that labor's voice is heard in any discussion about health care, retirement, and other worker issues. Without that voice, workers have no power at all.

Notes

1. Gail Shearer, "New Studies Show Administration Health Care Policy Will Divide Nation Into Healthy vs. Sick, Rich vs. Poor." July 15, 2004. www.consumersunion.org/pub/core-health-care/001248.html.
2. Study by the Commonwealth Fund, cited in Todd Zwillich, "Study Warns of High-Deductible Insurance Plans," *WebMD Medical News*, January 27, 2005. http://my.webmd.com/content/Article/100/105428.htm.

A Single-Payer System Will Be Good for American Business

Morton Minz

About the author: *Morton Minz covered the Supreme Court for the* Washington Post *from 1964 to 1965 and from 1977 to 1980. He is the former chair of the Fund for Investigative Journalism.*

B usiness leaders complain endlessly that the current system of private healthcare insurance based on employment provides fewer and fewer people with less and less quality care at higher and higher cost. Yet Corporate America turns its back on a publicly financed system, which, by all indicators, the taxpayers would willingly support.

Publicly financed but privately run healthcare for all—including free choice of physicians—would cost employers far less in taxes than their costs for insurance. Universal coverage could also work magic in less obvious ways. For example, employers would no longer have to pay for medical care under workers' compensation, which in 2002 cost them more than $38 billion. Auto-insurance rates would fall for them—and everyone—if the carriers were no longer liable for medical and hospital bills. You'd think that in its own selfish interest, Corporate America would be fighting to replace the existing system with universal health coverage. Yet it doesn't lift a finger.

The George W. Bush Administration's Health-Care Policy

Meanwhile, under the [George W.] Bush Administration healthcare coverage steadily shrinks. In 2000, according to the Census Bureau, 14 percent of Americans didn't have it; in 2003, 15.6 percent—45 million—did not. Actually, 85 million

Americans under age 65 were uninsured over varying periods during 2003–04, up from 81.8 million in 2002–03, according to Families USA, the consumer health organization. As more and more Americans become uninsured, spending on health-care soars. By 2001 it accounted for 13.9 percent of US gross domestic product. (It constituted a much smaller share of GDP [gross domestic product] in countries with universal healthcare, such as Sweden, 8.7 percent; France, 9.5 percent; and Canada, 9.7 percent.) Average family premiums in 2005 [were] projected to be $12,485, up $1,768 from 2004. The federal Centers for Medicare & Medicaid Services expects health-care outlays to rise from $1.8 trillion in 2004 to $2.7 trillion in 2010, nearly a trillion-dollar increase in six years. The forecast reflects annual increases of 14 percent to 18 percent. David Walker, head of the Government Accountability Office (GAO), the auditing arm of Congress, calls them "unsustainable."

Unaffordable Health Care Hurts Businesses

A simple fact largely explains why spending bloats while the ranks of the insured thin: Health insurance is increasingly un-affordable. After rising 38 percent between 2000 and the last quarter of 2003, the costs of providing healthcare to employees rose 11.2 percent between January and May of 2004, according to the Kaiser Family Foundation's annual survey of 3,000 companies. "Close to 75 percent of 205 senior-level executives surveyed [in May [2004]] by the Detroit Regional Chamber rank employee health insurance as 'unaffordable' and 25 percent consider it 'very unaffordable,'" the *Detroit News* reported. The Kaiser Family Foundation says that from 2001 to 2004 the proportion of workers receiving health coverage on the job dropped from 65 percent to 61 percent, a loss of 5 million jobs with health benefits. . . .

Reacting to rising expenditures on insurance, corporate managements' cut back on employee health benefits, triggering worker unrest. Consider the [a recent] five-month strike against supermarket chains in Southern California—the longest in the industry's history. It left about 60,000 union workers jobless, and it seriously hurt the owners as well. The central issue—in a state where half of all personal bankruptcies are related to medical bills—was the demand by Safeway, Kroger and Albertsons that members of the United Food and Commercial Workers (UFCW) union pay much more for health benefits. The settlement, reached [in] February [2004], sent a grim message to grocery workers everywhere.

Business leaders worship marketplace ideology "almost like religion. . . . It's emotional," says Raymond Werntz.

The strike "would not have occurred if we had a system of universal healthcare coverage," Greg Denier, assistant to the international president of the UFCW, told me. "All of our strikes in the past decade have occurred because of the absence of universal healthcare." Moreover, universal health coverage would have narrowed the wide gap in operating costs between the unionized chains and nonunion competitors, particularly 800-pound gorilla Wal-Mart. Unlike the chains, the world's biggest retailer charges so much for miserly health insurance that more than 60 percent of its poorly paid employees (averaging $8 an hour) don't buy it. Denier saw the strike as a symptom of "the slow-motion collapse of the employment-based healthcare system."

Leveling the Playing Field

Lawyer Harry Burton represented Safeway and Giant Food in subsequent negotiations with the UFCW in the Washington, DC, region. Speaking "as an individual," he essentially agreed with Denier. Universal health insurance would have "a profound effect" not just on the supermarket industry but "on nearly all collective bargaining." . . . Nonunion companies "virtually never" provide healthcare of the same quality as that provided by unionized competitors, thus creating "a vast disparity in costs." That's why a tax-supported national system would result in "a leveling of the playing field." I asked Burton what explains the resistance or indifference of employers to universal health insurance. "Very frequently it's ideology," he replied.

Business leaders worship marketplace ideology "almost like religion," says Raymond Werntz, who for nearly thirty years ran healthcare programs for Whitman Corporation, a Chicago-based multinational holding company. "It's emotional." In 1999 Werntz became the first president of the Consumer Health Education Council in Washington, a program of the Employee Benefit Research Institute, a nonprofit, nonpartisan group. He saw it as his mission to try to persuade employers to face the "huge, huge" issue of the uninsured because . . . "business has to be involved with the solution." The problem that emerged was its "unwillingness to even think about a solution." Last year, after funding ran out, a disappointed Werntz became the council's last and only president. . . .

[In Canada] single-payer [health insurance] "significantly reduces total labour costs . . . compared to the cost of equivalent private insurance purchased by US-based automakers."

The Canadian Model: Good for Business

Canada has had a single-payer system for more than thirty years (Australia, Denmark, Finland, Iceland, Sweden and Taiwan also have one.) American executives who have run Canadian subsidiaries see it as a business boon. Take General Motors [GM]. In 2003 its costs of building a midsize car in Canada were $1,400 less than building the identical car in the United States (the comparable figures for DaimlerChrysler and Ford were $1,300 and $1,200). Such savings are no mystery. Canadian companies pay far less in taxes for health coverage for everyone than the premiums they would pay under the US system to provide their employees with comparable benefits.

Highly placed Canadian business executives affirm that single-payer nurtures free enterprise. A. Charles Baillie, while chairman and CEO [chief executive officer] of Toronto Dominion Bank, one of Canada's six largest, hailed it in 1999 as "an economic asset, not a burden." He told the Vancouver Board of Trade, "In an era of globalization, we need every competitive and comparative advantage we have. And the fundamentals of our health care system are one of those advantages." He added: "The fact is, the free market . . . cannot work in the context of universal health care. While health care could be purchased like any other form of insurance . . . the risk and resource equation will always be such that, in some cases, demand will not be matched by supply. In other words, some people will always be left out." (A recent report by the World Bank ranked welfare states like Denmark, Finland and Sweden high in international competitiveness. An author of the study said; "Social protection is good for business, it takes the burden off of businesses for health care costs.")

Single-payer or other fundamental healthcare reforms stall unless backed by the business organizations that govern the government.

In 2002, top executives of the Big Three automakers' Canadian units joined Basil (Buzz) Hargrove, president of the Canadian Auto Workers (CAW) union, in signing a "Joint Letter on Publicly Funded Health Care." At a press conference with Hargrove, Michael Grimaldi, president and general manager of GM Canada and a GM vice president, called single-payer "a strategic advantage for Canada." The joint letter, also signed by Ford's and DaimlerChrysler's presidents and CEOs,

Alain Batty and Ed Brust, said that while providing "essential and affordable healthcare services for all," single-payer "significantly reduces total labour costs ... compared to the cost of equivalent private insurance services purchased by US-based automakers" and "has been an important ingredient" in the success of Canada's "most important export industry." The *Toronto Star* explained how the CAW used "credible corporate data" to quantify "the competitive advantage that [single-payer] provides to the Canadian auto industry. The union compared the hourly labour costs of vehicle assembly in Canada and the United States. The Canadian rate, including wages, benefits and payroll taxes, was $29.90 per hour. The American rate was $45.60. (All figures are in US dollars.) Healthcare accounted for more than a quarter of the difference. It saved Canadian employers $4 per hour per worker." Monthly health-coverage costs for Canadian employers average about $50, mostly for items such as eyeglasses and orthopedic shoes: health-insurance costs for US employers average *$552*, the *Washington Post* has reported. . . .

Resistance from Employers

No matter how urgently needed, no matter how common-sensical, no matter how much bottom lines would be fattened, single-payer or other fundamental healthcare reforms stall unless backed by the business organizations that govern the government. The Clinton Administration learned this to its sorrow after proposing its complex, comprehensive plan.[1] Business organizations "effectively killed the bill," Walter Maher, former vice president for public policy of Daimler-Chrysler, wrote ... in the *American Journal of Public Health* [2003]. The bill aroused formidable opposition from businesses such as fast-food chains like McDonald's. It mostly hired young people, worked them less than full time, paid them little and provided scant if any health coverage. Of the

1. In 1993–1994 the Clinton Administration attempted to create a universal-coverage plan for all Americans. The plan died in Congress.

PepsiCo chains' hourly employees, a survey indicated, 71 percent were covered by someone else's health insurance. If that someone was a parent employed by, say, an automaker facing global competition, the manufacturer was effectively subsidizing chains that had no such competition. Free-riding defeated a primary goal of the bill, which was to spread healthcare costs throughout the economy by letting no employers escape paying their fair share.

The bill received a big boost when the US Chamber of Commerce and the National Association of Manufacturers (NAM) let pragmatism trump ideology and endorsed it. And the mighty Business Roundtable (BRT), an association of 150 CEOs of the country's biggest corporations, with multitrillion-dollar revenues, was "at least prepared not to oppose" the mandate. . . .

But insurers and other businesses that profited from preserving the healthcare status quo exerted fierce counterpressures. The Chamber "suddenly reversed course and totally rejected the Clinton Plan," Maher wrote. The NAM abruptly withdrew its endorsement six weeks after granting it. At the BRT several politically powerful members, including the CEOs of eight major and a few lesser pharmaceutical manufacturers, and of a dozen insurers and healthcare providers, opposed the bill. It got only a single vote—Chrysler's, Maher told me. "It's definitely fair to say that CEOs are very reluctant to take unpopular positions against their colleagues in the BRT," he added. "If a huge majority of them are staunch conservatives who have no interest in health reform, or in using the government to control costs, or to expand coverage, or even to moderate health costs using regulatory tools, it'll be a rare CEO who will want to take on his CEO buddies. That's absolutely true."

Today, BRT executive director Patricia Hanahan Engman contends that "public financing cannot provide the same level of quality doctors, hospitals and prescription drugs generated by the competition inherent in the private market." She should tell that to GM president and CEO G. Richard Wagoner Jr. Judged by sixteen top health indicators, he said in June [2005], the United States ranks twelfth among thirteen industrialized countries. "It will be a cold day in hell when the BRT leads the charge for universal health coverage in the United States," Maher told me.

Let's Provide Medicare for All Americans

Pete Stark

About the author*: Pete Stark, ranking Democrat on the House Ways and Means Health Subcommittee, has represented California's 13th District since 1973.*

It's no secret that the healthcare system is sick. To maximize profits and shareholder confidence, insurance companies, healthcare providers and drug companies have manipulated the system beyond comprehension. As healthcare costs rise at double-digit rates, fewer and fewer manufacturers and small businesses can offer comprehensive coverage to their employees. General Motors recently admitted it spends more on healthcare than on steel; Starbucks spends more on health insurance than on coffee. And those problems do not even begin to speak to the needs of the uninsured—all 46 million of them, including 9 million children.

Thankfully, the cure is not nearly as complicated as the disease. There is a road map laid out for us: a program that already delivers universal healthcare to nearly 42 million Americans. And it is simple: Workers pay into the system while they're young, and when they turn 65 the government pays their health insurance.

The program, of course, is Medicare. Medicare has lower administrative costs than any private plan on the market. It enjoys one of the highest approval ratings of any government program. But the most important reason Medicare is the best model for an expansion of healthcare benefits is that the program focuses on patients, not profits.

Healthcare gets complicated when it's built around profits rather than care. With patient-first simplicity in mind, I have introduced two proposals to deliver quality, affordable healthcare to every American. First is MediKids, a plan to provide universal coverage to children from birth to age 23. Children would be automatically enrolled at birth, with parents having the choice to opt out of the program by enrolling their children in private plans or in other government programs. But if lapse in other insurance coverage were to occur, MediKids would automatically pick up the child's health insurance. Simple.

With Medicare as a model, we can fill the growing gaps in health coverage and ultimately weave together a stable, comprehensive, affordable system for Americans.

So is the Medicare Early Access Act. This measure would allow people to buy into Medicare once they turn 55—providing essential help to the 4 million uninsured Americans over age 54 who are not currently eligible. To make their premiums affordable, enrollees would receive a tax credit to cover 75 percent of the cost.

These proposals are only a beginning. With Medicare as a model, we can fill the growing gaps in health coverage and ultimately weave together a stable, comprehensive, affordable system for Americans of all ages. Medicare has shown us the power of simplicity; we need only expand its promise to the rest of our population.

Glossary

associated health plan A proposed plan that would allow small employers, on statewide bases, to aggregate their employees into a single health-care plan that could lower expenses for both employers and employees. As of 2006, this organizational plan had not received congressional approval, chiefly because it would have voided specific state-mandated provisions for coverage.

benefit The reimbursement a member receives for covered medical expenses that are specified in his or her insurance plan.

carrier The insurance company or HMO (see below) that insures a specific health plan.

claim A formal request made by an insured person for the benefits provided by his or her policy.

co-pay(ment) The amount an insured person must pay toward the cost of a particular benefit. For example, a plan might require a $15 co-pay for each doctor's office visit or a $5 co-payment for a prescription.

deductible The amount an insured individual must pay for covered expenses during each calendar year before his or her health plan begins to pay for specified benefits.

fee-for-service The traditional way of paying for medical care: direct payment for services rendered, whether to a physician, physical therapist, hospital, etc.

gatekeeper An individual—in the case of health insurance, usually a case manager, benefits manager, or primary-care physician—who decides if an insured person will be covered by insurance benefits while going outside the system or consulting a specialist within the system of care; the goal is to contain costs.

generic drug A chemical equivalent to a brand-name (patented) drug. Such drugs cost less, and the savings are passed on to health plan members in the form of lower co-pays. Because generic drugs may use different binders along with their therapeutically active ingredients, they may not react in precisely the same ways as brand-name pharmaceuticals—sometimes a point of contention between health-care activists and health-care providers.

HMO [Health Maintenance Organization] A form of health care first organized in the 1910–1920s, in which occupational groups spend their health-care dollars to build systems that employ physicians and other **providers**, including hospitals, that in turn offer services to members. Such systems were strengthened in the 1970s and became, by the 1980s, the dominant form of health-care provision in the United States. HMOs stress preventive care, early diagnosis, and treatment on an outpatient basis. HMOs are licensed by each state to provide care for enrollees by contracting with specific health-care providers to provide specified benefits. Most HMOs require enrollees to see a particular **primary-care physician (PCP)**, who acts as a **gatekeeper** to control members' access to specialists, hospitalization, and other services.

HSA [Health Savings Account] Health Savings Accounts (HSAs) were created by the Medicare bill signed by President George W. Bush on December 8, 2003, and are designed to help individuals save for future qualified medical and retiree health expenses on a tax-free basis. Contributions to tax-free HSAs can be made by employers, employees, and other individuals as long as they also hold high-deductible health plans and have no other first-dollar coverage. The money can be withdrawn, tax-free, to cover medical expenses. These accounts have replaced **Medical Savings Accounts**, an earlier form of similar health insurance.

Hillary-care A term used by conservative and libertarian health-care policy analysts and legislators. So-named for Hillary Rodham Clinton, who spearheaded the 1993–1994 effort by the Clinton administration to create universal coverage for American citizens. The effort failed for a variety of reasons: great complexity and resistance on the part of the U.S. health insurance industry and Republicans in Congress.

MSA [Medical Savings Account] A market-driven scheme in which individuals could save money toward high-deductible medical expenses in tax-free savings accounts until they had use of them. Superseded by HSAs in 2003.

managed care The coordination of health-care services in the attempt to produce high-quality health-care for the lowest possible cost. Examples are the use of primary care physicians as gatekeepers in HMO plans and pre-certification of care.

Medicaid The federally created health-coverage plan for indigent people created by Congress in 1965. Medicaid depends on a combination of contributions from state and federal governments; its benefits and coverage are constantly changing as state and federal government contributions change.

Medicare The federally created health-coverage plan for people over 65 and disabled people created by Congress in 1965. Medicare depends on federal contributions; its benefits and coverage change constantly as federal policy and funding on Medicare shift.

network A group of doctors, hospitals and other providers contracted to provide services to insured individuals for less than their usual fees. Provider networks can cover large geographic markets and/or a wide range of health-care services. If a health plan uses a preferred provider network, insured individuals typically pay less for using a network provider.

out-of-network A provider or health-care facility which is not part of a health plan's network. Insured individuals usually pay more when using an out-of-network provider, if the plan uses a network.

out-of-pocket maximum The total of an insured individual's co-insurance payments and co-payments.

PCC [Primary Care Physician] In HMOs, the **gatekeeper provider** for members of the HMO; this physician determines whether or not the individual can go **out-of-network** or advance to seeing a specialist within the system. This function is designed to keep costs down.

PPO [Preferred Provider Organization] A network or group of physicians and hospitals that agrees to discount its normal fees in exchange for a high volume of patients. Insured individuals can choose from among the physicians within the network; to see physicians outside it, they must consult their **primary care physician**, who acts as **gatekeeper** to other, and more costly, providers.

provider Any person or entity providing health care services, including hospitals, physicians, home health agencies and nursing homes. Usually licensed by the state.

single-payer A system of health-care provisions that uses only a single administrative entity to determine eligibility, pay claims, and handle other administrative duties. Most commonly, a federal government.

third-party payer An organization responsible for marketing and administering small group and individual health plans.

Its functions include collecting premiums, paying claims, providing administrative services, and promoting the services and products available through the plan(s).

Organizations to Contact

The editors have compiled the following list of organizations concerned with the issues debated in this book. The descriptions are derived from materials provided by the organizations. All have publications or information available for interested readers. The list was compiled when the present volume was published; the information provided here may have changed since then. Be aware that many organizations take several weeks or longer to respond to inquiries, so allow as much time as possible.

American Association of Retired Persons (AARP)
601 E St. NW, Washington, DC   20049
(800) 424-3410
Web site: www.aarp.org

AARP is a nonprofit, nonpartisan membership organization for people 50 and over. It provides information and resources; advocates on legislative, consumer, and legal issues; assists members to serve their communities; and offers a wide range of unique benefits, special products, and services for members. These benefits include *AARP The Magazine*, the monthly *AARP Bulletin*, and the Spanish language newspaper, *AARP Segunda Juventud*. Active in every state, the District of Columbia, Puerto Rico, and the U.S. Virgin Islands, AARP celebrates the attitude that age is just a number and life is what you make it.

American Enterprise Institute (AEI)
1150 17th St. NW, Washington, DC   20036
(202) 862-5800 • fax: (202) 862-7178
Web site: www.aei.org

The American Enterprise Institute for Public Policy Research is dedicated to preserving and strengthening the foundations of freedom—limited government, private enterprise, vital cultural and political institutions, and a strong foreign policy and national defense—through scholarly research, open debate, and publications. Founded in 1943, AEI researches economics and trade; social welfare and health; government tax, spending, regulatory, and legal policies; U.S. politics; international affairs; and U.S. defense and foreign policies. The institute publishes dozens of books and hundreds of articles and reports each year and a policy magazine, the *American Enterprise.*

American Society of Law, Medicine & Ethics (ASLME)

765 Commonwealth Ave., Suite 1634, Boston, MA   02215
(617) 262-4990 • fax: (617) 437-7596
e-mail: info@aslme.org
Web site: www.aslme.org

The mission of ASLME is to provide high-quality scholarship, debate, and critical thought to professionals in the fields of law, health-care policy, and ethics. The society acts as a source of guidance and information through the publication of two quarterlies, the *Journal of Law, Medicine & Ethics* and the *American Journal of Law & Medicine.*

Brookings Institution

1775 Massachusetts Ave. NW, Washington, DC   20036-2188
(202) 797-6105 • fax: (202) 797-2495
Web site: www.brook.edu

Founded in 1927, the institution is a liberal research and education organization that publishes material on economics, government, and foreign policy. It strives to serve as a bridge between scholarship and public policy, bringing new knowledge to the attention of decision makers and providing scholars with improved insight into public policy issues. The Brookings Institution produces hundreds of abstracts and reports on health care with topics ranging from Medicaid to persons with disabilities.

Cato Institute

1000 Massachusetts Ave. NW, Washington, DC   20001-5403
(202) 842-0200 • fax: (202) 842-3490
e-mail: cato@cato.org
Web site: www.cato.org

The institute is a libertarian public policy research foundation dedicated to limiting the role of government and protecting individual liberties. Its Health and Welfare Studies department works to formulate and popularize a free-market agenda for health-care reform. The institute publishes the quarterly magazine *Regulation*, the bimonthly *Cato Policy Report*, and numerous books and commentaries, hundreds of which relate to health care.

Center for Economic and Social Rights (CESR)

162 Montague St., 3rd Floor, Brooklyn, NY   11201
(718) 237-9145 • fax: (718) 237-9147
e-mail: rights@cesr.org
Web site: www.cesr.org

Established in 1993, CESR is one of the first organizations to challenge economic injustice as a violation of international human rights law. Through its projects abroad and in the United States, CESR has developed an effective strategy that combines research, advocacy, collaboration, and education. CESR believes that economic and social rights—legally binding on all nations—can provide a universally accepted framework for strengthening social justice activism.

Center for Studying Health System Change (HSC)

600 Maryland Ave. SW, #550, Washington, DC   20024
(202) 484-5261 • fax: (202) 484-9258
Web site: www.hschange.com

The Center for Studying Health System Change is a nonpartisan policy research organization. HSC designs and conducts studies focused on the U.S. health-care system to inform the thinking and decisions of policy makers in government and private industry. In addition to this applied use, HSC studies contribute more broadly to the body of health-care policy research that enables decision makers to understand changes to the health-care system and the national and local market forces driving those changes. It publishes issue briefs, community reports, tracking reports, data bulletins, and journal articles based on its research.

Commonwealth Fund

1 E. 75th St., New York, NY 10021
(212) 606-3800 • fax: (212) 606-3500
e-mail: cmwf@cmwf.org
Web site: www.cmwf.org

The Commonwealth Fund is a private foundation that aims to promote a high performing health-care system that achieves better access, improved quality, and greater efficiency, particularly for society's most vulnerable, including low-income people, the uninsured, minority Americans, young children, and elderly adults. The fund carries out this mandate by supporting independent research on health-care issues and making grants to improve health-care practice and policy. An international program in health policy is designed to stimulate innovative policies and practices in the United States and other industrialized countries.

Healthcare Leadership Council (HLC)

900 17th St. NW, Suite 600, Washington, DC 20006
(202) 452-8700
Web site: www.hlc.org

The council is a forum in which health care industry leaders can jointly develop policies, plans, and programs that support a market-based health-care system. HLC believes America's health-care system should value innovation and provide affordable high-quality health care free from excessive government regulations. It offers the latest press releases on health issues and several public policy papers with titles such as "Empowering Consumers and Patients" and "Ensuring Responsible Government."

Heritage Foundation
214 Massachusetts Ave. NE, Washington, DC   20002-4999
(800) 544-4843 • fax: (202) 544-6979
e-mail: pubs@heritage.org
Web site: www.heritage.org

The foundation is a public policy research institute that advocates limited government and the free market system. It believes the private sector, not government, should be relied upon to ease social problems. The Heritage Foundation publishes the quarterly *Policy Review*, as well as hundreds of monographs, books, and background papers with titles such as *Medicare Minus Choice* and *What to Do About Uninsured Children*.

Hoover Institution
Stanford University, Stanford, CA   94305-6010
(650) 723-1754 • fax: (650) 723-1687
e-mail: horaney@hoover.stanford.edu
Web site: www.hoover.org

The Hoover Institution on War, Revolution and Peace, Stanford University, is a public policy research center devoted to the advanced study of politics, economics, and political economy—both domestic and foreign—as well as international affairs. With its world-renowned group of scholars and ongoing programs of policy-oriented research, the Hoover Institution puts its accumulated knowledge to work as a prominent contributor to the world marketplace of ideas defining a free society.

Institute for Health Freedom (IHF)
1825 Eye Street NW, Suite 500, Washington, DC   20036
(202) 429-6610 • fax: (202) 861-1973
e-mail: ForHealthFreedom.org
Web site: www.forhealthfreedom.org

The institute is a nonpartisan, nonprofit research center established to bring the issues of personal freedom in choosing health care to the forefront of America's health policy debate.

Its mission is to present the ethical and economic case for strengthening personal health freedom. IHF's research and analyses are published as policy briefings, including "Children's Health Care," "Monopoly in Medicine," and "Legal Issues." All are available through its Web site.

Institute of Medicine
500 5th St. NW, Washington, DC   20001
(202) 334-2352 • fax: (202) 334-1412
e-mail: iomwww@nas.edu
Web site: www.iom.edu

The Institute of Medicine serves as adviser to the nation to improve health. Established in 1970 under the charter of the National Academy of Sciences, the Institute of Medicine provides independent, objective, evidence-based advice to policy makers, health professionals, the private sector, and the public. Many of its studies are available online at its Web site.

Henry J. Kaiser Family Foundation [KFF]
2400 Sand Hill Road, Menlo Park, CA   94025
(650) 854-9400 • fax: (650) 854-4800
Web site: www.kff.org

The Henry J. Kaiser Family Foundation is a non profit, private operating foundation focusing on the major health-care issues facing the nation. The foundation is an independent voice and source of facts and analysis for policy makers, the media, the health-care community, and the general public. KFF develops and runs its own research and communications programs, often in partnership with outside organizations. The foundation contracts with a wide range of outside individuals and organizations through its programs. Through its policy research and communications programs, it works to provide reliable information in a health system in which the issues are increasingly complex and the nation faces difficult challenges and choices. The foundation is not associated with Kaiser Permanente or Kaiser Industries.

National Center for Policy Analysis (NCPA)
655 15th St. NW, Suite 375, Washington, DC   20005
(202) 628-6671 • fax: (202) 628-6474
e-mail: ncpa@public-policy.org
Web site: www.ncpa.org

NCPA is a nonprofit public policy research institute. It publishes the bimonthly newsletter *Executive Alert* as well as numerous health-care policy studies, including "Saving Medicare" and "Medical Savings Accounts: Obstacles to Their Growth and Ways to Improve Them," and its Web site includes an extensive section on health-care issues.

National Coalition on Health Care (NCHC)
1200 G St. NW, Suite 750, Washington, DC   20005
(202) 638-7151 • fax: (202) 638-7166
e-mail: cfitzpatrick@nchc.org
Web site: www.nchc.org

NCHC is a nonprofit, nonpartisan group that represents the nation's largest alliance working to improve America's health care and make it more affordable. The coalition offers several policy studies, including "Why the Quality of U.S. Health Care Must Be Improved" and "The Rising Number of Uninsured Workers: An Approaching Crisis in Health Care Financing."

National Medical Association (NMA)
1012 10th St. NW, Washington, DC   20001
(202) 347-1895 • fax: (202) 898-2510
e-mail: HealthPolicy@nmanet.org
Web site: www.nmanet.org

NMA is the collective voice of African American physicians and the leading force for parity and justice in medicine and the elimination of disparities in health. NMA is the largest and oldest national organization representing African American physicians and their patients in the United States. NMA represents the interests of more than 25,000 African American physicians and the patients they serve. NMA is committed to improving the quality of health among minorities and disadvantaged people through its membership, professional development, community health education, advocacy, research and partnerships with federal and private agencies. Throughout its history the NMA has focused primarily on health issues related to African Americans and medically underserved populations; however, its principles, goals, initiatives and philosophy encompass all ethnic groups.

Physicians for a National Health Program (PNHP)

29 E Madison, Suite 602, Chicago, IL   60602
(312) 782-6006 • fax: (312) 782-6007
e-mail: pnhp@aol.com
Web site: www.pnhp.org

PNHP is a single-issue organization advocating a universal, comprehensive single-payer national health program. PNHP has more than 14,000 members and chapters across the United States. Its members and physician activists work toward a single-payer national health program in their communities. PNHP organizes rallies, town hall meetings, and debates; coordinates speakers and forum discussions; contributes op-eds and articles to the nation's top newspapers, medical journals, and magazines; and appears regularly on national television and news programs advocating for a single-payer system.

Project EINO (Everybody In, Nobody Out)

1815 MLK Parkway, Suite 2, PMB 142, Durham, NC   27707
(919) 402-0133
Web site: www.righttohealthcare.org

The mission of Project EINO and RightToHealthCare.org is to provide educational resources and a forum for discussion on the concept of a right to health care. This educational work includes the history and philosophy of the concept and its relation to other human rights, legal documentation and argumentation, the geography of work on the right to health care, the relation of this concept to other work in U.S. health care reform, and international perspectives. EINO provides a Web-based discussion forum including opposing viewpoints to assist visitors in evaluating the issues from all perspectives. The educational work is intended to provide a basis for broad popular mobilization, demands on legislatures, and activism on this issue.

RAND Corporation
1776 Main St., Santa Monica, CA   90401-3208
(310) 393-0411 • fax: (310) 393-4818
Web site: www.rand.org

The RAND Corporation is a nonprofit institution that for almost 60 years has helped improve policy and decision making through research and analysis. Initially, RAND focused on issues of national security. Eventually, it expanded its intellectual reserves to offer insight into other areas, such as business, education, health, law, and science. Today, RAND emphasizes areas of research that reflect the changing nature of a global society. Much of this research is carried out on behalf of public and private sponsors and clients. RAND also conducts its own RAND-initiated research on issues that otherwise might not receive funding. RAND communicates its findings to a wide audience through announcements to media, testimony by experts at RAND (often to the U.S. Congress), and publications, many of which are available free on its Web site.

Urban Institute
2100 M St. NW, Washington, DC   20037
(202) 261-5244
Web site: www.urban.org

The Urban Institute investigates social and economic problems confronting the nation and analyzes efforts to solve these problems. It also works to improve government decisions and to increase citizens' awareness about important public choices. It offers a wide variety of resources, including books such as *Restructuring Medicare: Impacts on Beneficiaries* and *The Decline in Medical Spending Growth in 1996: Why Did It Happen?*

Bibliography

Books

Henry J. Aaron and William B. Schwartz, with Melissa Cox
Can We Say No? The Challenge of Rationing Health Care. Washington, DC: Brookings Institution, 2005.

Ronald J. Angel, Laura Lein, and Jane Henrici
Poor Families in America's Health Care Crisis. New York: Cambridge University Press, 2006.

Michael F. Cannon and Michael D. Tanner
Healthy Competition: What's Holding Back Health Care and How to Free It. Washington, DC: Cato Institute, 2005.

John F. Cogan, R. Glenn Hubbard, and Daniel P. Kessler
Healthy, Wealthy, and Wise: Five Steps to a Better Health Care System. Washington, DC: AEI Press, 2005.

Jan Gregoire Coombs
The Rise and Fall of HMOs: An American Health Care Revolution. Madison: University of Wisconsin Press, 2005.

David M. Cutler
Your Money or Your Life: Strong Medicine for America's Health Care System. New York: Oxford University Press, 2004.

Philip J. Funigiello
Chronic Politics: Health Care Security from FDR to George W. Bush. Lawrence: University Press of Kansas, 2005.

Sherry Glied — *Chronic Condition: Why Health Reform Fails.* Cambridge, MA: Harvard University Press, 1997.

Dana P. Goldman and Elizabeth A. McGlynn — *U.S. Health Care: Facts About Costs, Access, and Quality.* Santa Monica, CA: RAND Health, 2005.

Merrill Goozer — *The $800 Million Pill: The Truth Behind the Cost of New Drugs.* Berkeley and Los Angeles: University of California Press, 2004.

Arnold Kling — *Crisis of Abundance: Rethinking How We Pay for Health Care.* Washington, DC: Cato Institute, 2006.

Ray Moynihan and Alan Cassels — *Selling Sickness: How the World's Biggest Pharmaceutical Companies are Turning Us All into Patients.* New York: Nation Books, 2005.

Michael E. Porter and Elizabeth Olmsted Teisberg — *Redefining Health Care: Creating Value-Based Competition on Results.* Cambridge, MA: Harvard Business School Press, 2006.

Susan Sered and Rushika Fernandopulle — *Uninsured in America: Life and Death in the Land of Opportunity.* Berkeley and Los Angeles: University of California Press, 2005.

United States Congress
Senate Special Committee on Aging. *America's Ailing Health Care System: Hearing before the Senate Special Committee on Aging, United States Senate, 108th Congress, first session.* Washington, DC: USGPO, 2003. http://purl.access.gpo.gov/GPO/LPS34042

United States Congress
Senate Committee on Small Business and Entrepreneurship. *The Small Business Health Care Crisis: Possible Solutions: Hearing before the Senate Committee on Small Business and Entrepreneurship, United States Senate, 108th Congress, first session.* Washington, DC: USGPO, 2004. http://purl.access.gpo.gov/GPO/LPS49215

Periodicals

Reed Abelson
"Wal-Mart's Health Care Struggle Is Corporate America's, Too," *New York Times,* October 29, 2005.

Marcia Angell
"Your Dangerous Drugstore," *New York Review of Books,* June 8, 2006.

Anon
"The Wal-Mart Tax: Shifting Health Care Costs to Taxpayers," *AFL-CIO online,* March 31, 2005. www.aflcio.org/corporatewatch/walmart/upload/walmart_tax_memo.pdf

John Breaux "Ceasefire on Health Care: A Centrist's Approach to Reform," *The Commonwealth Fund*, March 2006.

Ronald Brownstein "Healthcare Crisis Goes Untreated, but the Cancer Is Spreading," *Los Angeles Times*, October 3, 2005.

Michael F. Cannon "Health Care Needs a Dose of Competition," *Business Daily*, October 4, 2005.

Meredith Clark "Life Without Health Insurance," *The Nation Online*, February 3, 2005. www.thenation.com/doc/20050221/clark

Elaine Ditsler, Peter Fisher, and Colin Gordon "On the Fringe: The Substandard Benefits of Works in Part-Time, Temporary, and Contract Jobs," *The Commonwealth Fund*, December 2005.

European Union "Charter of Fundamental Rights of the European Union," *Official Journal* C364, December 18, 2000.

Bob Filner "Model Healthcare," *The Nation*, February 6, 2006.

Mary E. Forsberg "Attention Shoppers: You Pay the Health Insurance Bills For Some of New Jersey's Largest Employers," *New Jersey Policy Perspective*, August 2005.

David Gratzer "Putting Patients First: Bush's Health Care Agenda," *The Weekly Standard*, February 6, 2006.

Kaiser Family Foundation — "Health Costs and Budgets," statehealthfacts.org [accessed August 21, 2006]. www.statehealthfacts.org/cgibin/healthfacts.cgi?action=compare &category=Health+Cost s+%26+ Budgets&welcome=1

David Kelley — "Is There a Right to Health Care?" *The Objectivist.* n.d. [2005] www.objectivistcenter.org

Marsha Lillie-Blanton, Rose Marie Martinez, and Alina Salganicoff — "Site of Medical Care: Do Racial and Ethnic Differences Persist?" http://academic.udayton.edu/health/03access/access01.htm

M. Merlin, D. Gould, and B. Mahato — "Rising Out-of-Pocket Spending for Medical Care: A Growing Strain on Family Budgets," *The Commonwealth Fund*, February 2006.

National Medical Association — "Where the NMA Stands on Key Health Policy Issues," *NMA Online*, October 29, 2005.

David Phelps — "HMOs Steadily Losing Ground," *Minneapolis Star Tribune*, August 25, 2006. D1, D6.

Alan Reynolds — "Wal-Mart Health Benefit Blues," *Washington Times*, February 26, 2006.

Mitt Romney — "Health Care for Everyone? We've Found a Way," *Wall Street Journal*, April 11, 2006.

Wal-Mart Stores   "Wal-Mart's Health Care Benefits Are
                      Competitive in the Retail Sector,"
                      Wal-Mart Facts.com, January 2006.

Joel Wendland   "The Wal-Mart Health Care Crisis,"
                      Political Affairs Magazine, February
                      7–March 5, 2006.

Index

A

Abortion, 162
Accountability, 74, 165–168
    See also Personal responsibility
Administrative costs, 132, 184
Adverse selection, 173
American Association of Retired Persons (AARP), 191
American College of Physicians Foundation, 87
American Enterprise Institute (AEI), 191–192
American Medical Association (AMA), 78
American Society of Law, Medicine, & Ethics (ASLME), 192
Antihistamines, 90–91
Atlas, Scott W., 53, 96
Auto insurance rates, 176
Automakers, Canadian, 179–181

B

Baillie, A. Charles, 180
Balko, Radley, 165
Bankruptcies, 56–60, 178
Barnhill, Glen, 146
Batty, Alain, 181
Baucus, Max, 115
BidForSurgery.com, 94
Biotechnologies, 162
Blair, Tony, 43
Blood tests, 89
Blue Cross/Blue Shield, 102
Bredesen, Phil, 146, 147, 153–154
Brookings Institution, 192

Brown, Jerry, 165
Brust, Ed, 181
Bufwack, Mary, 150
Burton, Larry, 178
Bush administration
    anti-obesity proposal, 165
    Bush, George W., 51, 63, 100
    health care policy of, 100, 125–126, 130, 132–133, 156, 174, 176–177
    Medicare Act of 2003, 97–98
    prescription drug program, 133
    promotion of HSAs by, 78, 159, 174
    response of, to Hurricane Katrina, 111, 115–117
Business Roundtable (BRT), 182–183
Businesses
    health-care expenditures by, 16–17
    single-payer system would benefit, 176–183
    See also Employers

C

Camalt, Jean, 23
Canadian health care system
    business and, 179–181
    percent of GDP in, 132
    problems with, 41–44
Cannon, Michael F., 158
Cash and Counseling Program, 118–119
Cato Institute, 193
Center for Economic and Social Rights (CESR), 23, 193

Center for Health Services Research, 150

Center for Health Transformation, 74

Center for Medicare & Medicaid Services (CMS), 115

Center for Studying Health System Change (HSC), 193–194

Chamberlain, Kathy, 149

Chaoulli, Jacques, 42

Charter of Fundamental Rights, 21

Children, universal coverage for, 185

Chronic conditions
health care tailored to, 103–104
self-monitoring of, 91–92, 104

Clark, Cindy, 150

Clinton administration, 35, 181

Clinton, Bill, 123, 148

Clinton, Hillary, 100, 166

Cogan, John, 48, 125–126

Cold War propaganda, 25–26

Collins, Sara R., 120

Common good, 157

Commonwealth Fund, 120, 194

Community-level health markets, 65–68

Comparison shopping, for drugs, 91

Competition
in health care industry, 62–63, 104–105
for specialty services, 66

Computerized tomography (CT) scans, 18

Conover, Christopher, 54, 106, 159

Conservative view
health care reform, 78–79, 156–157
right to health care, 22

U.S. health care system, 46–47, 48–52

Constitutional amendment, to guarantee health care, 27–31

Consumer Health Education Council, 179

Consumer-driven health care
concept of, 69–70, 81
differences in, 81–82
erodes health care for all Americans, 123–128
growth of, 63–65
increased need for patient information in, 139–141
is not answer to health care crisis, 142–145
is not effective, 120–122
legal obstacles to self-care and, 92–95
patient access to medical information and, 82–83
patient care management and, 86–92
patient-ordered tests and, 88–90
personal responsibility and, 170–171
prompts less spending, 81–92
rejection of, 79–80
will not reduce costs, 129–133
See also Health savings accounts (HSAs); High-deductible health plans (HDHPs)

Consumer-driven health plans (CDHPs)
affect of, on patient spending, 138–139
establishment of, 78
need for patient information and, 139–141
selection effects, 138
See also High-deductible health plans (HDHPs)

Consumers
  HSAs empower, 100–101
  informed choice by, 156–157
  See also Patients
Corney, Bob, 153

D

Damberg, Cheryl, 134
Dappen, Alan, 88
Declaration of Independence, 39
Deductibles
  high, 173
  increases in, 85–86
  raising, reduces costs, 96–99
  See also High-deductible
    health plans (HDHPs)
Defensive medicine, 74
Denier, Greg, 178
Deregulation, 53–55, 106–110
Direct-to-consumer advertising, 83
Discontinuity of care, 103
Doctors. *See* Physicians
Drescher, Michael, 149, 154
Drug advertising, 83
Drugs
  comparison shopping for, 91
  generic, 138
  over-the-counter (OTC), 90–
    91, 94
  prescription, 94, 133
  Rx-to-OTC switching, 94
Dunn, Wayne, 35

E

Ear infections, 89
EarCheck Middle Ear Monitor, 89
Economic Report of the President
  (2004), 125–126, 127
E-mail consultations, 87–88, 95
Emergency contraception, 162

Emergency Health Care Relief Act,
  115–116
Employee Benefit Research Institute, 120
Employees, shifting of health costs
  to, 85–86, 169–175
Employers
  deposits into HSAs by, 103–
    104
  resistance to universal health
    care among, 181–183
  shifting of health costs to em-
    ployees by, 85–86, 169–175
Employer-sponsored health insurance
  changes in, 102–103
  drop in, 17–18, 169–170, 177–
    178
  history of U.S., 17
  increasing cost of, 63–64, 123–
    124
  local market pressures and,
    68–69
  tax code and, 101–102, 163
England, private care in, 43
Engman, Patricia Hanahan, 182–
  183
Ethical values, 161, 162
European Union (EU)
  Charter of Fundamental
    Rights, 21
  private care in, 43
Evans, Tim, 43

F

Families, health-care expenditures
  by, 16, 85–86, 177
Federal Employees Health Benefits
  Program, 33–34
Federal Medical Assistance Per-
  centage (FMAP), 115
Feldstein, Martin, 159

First Health Services Corporation, 148

Florida Medicaid program, 152

Food and Drug Administration (FDA), 94, 107, 108

France, 132

Francis, David R., 142

Frist, Bill, 147

Fronstin, Paul, 120

G

General Motors, 16–17, 124, 179–180, 183, 184

Generic drugs, 138

Genetic engineering, 162

Genetic tests, 89

Gingrich, Newt, 74

Ginsburg, Paul B., 61

Goldman, Dana, 137

Goodman, John C., 100

Government regulations
   costs of, 105, 106–110, 159
   on drugs, 94
   on health care, 18, 22
   on physician licensing, 92–93
   reduction of, 79
   on referrals, 93–94
   should be reduced, 53–55

Government-sponsored health care. *See* Universal health care

Grassley, Charles, 115

Gratzer, David, 41

Great Society programs, 78, 147

Grimaldi, Michael, 180

H

Hargrove, Basil, 180

Harkin, Tom, 32

Health care
   as basic human right, 21–26, 32–34

constitutional amendment to guarantee, 27–31

is not a right, 35–40

market models do not apply to, 142–145

personal responsibility for, 165–169, 170–171

Health care costs
   consumer-driven care will not reduce, 129–133
   employer-provided plans and rising, 123–124
   government control of, 53–54
   high-deductible plans lower, 96–99
   increases in, 61–65, 142–143
   reasons for high, 131
   shifting of, to employees, 85–86, 169–175

Health care industry
   competition in, 62–63
   deregulation, 53–55, 106–110
   on local level, 65–68
   regulation of, 22
   state mandates on, 79

Health care reform
   conservative views of, 78–79, 156–157
   debate over, 46–47, 78–80
   deregulation, 53–55, 106–110
   individual decision-making and, 160–164
   liberal views on, 79–80, 157
   of Medicaid, 111–119
   physicians' recommendations for, 75–76
   privatization, 100–105
   tax code and, 48–52, 79, 101–102, 163
   values-driven, 160–164

Health care system. *See* U.S. health care system

Health Insurance Experiment (HIE), 135–136

Health insurance industry
  consumer distrust of, 85
  deregulation of, 105
  national market of, 104–105, 163–164
  rate increases in, 16
Health insurance plans, personal and portable, 102–103
Health maintenance organization (HMOs)
  establishment of, 78
  increasing costs and, 18
  TennCare and, 148
Health reimbursement arrangements (HRAs), 81, 120, 134
Health savings accounts (HSAs)
  affect of, on patient spending, 138–139
  are not effective, 120–122
  chronic illness and, 103–104
  consumer-driven care and, 81, 134
  criticisms of, 79
  disadvantages of, 126–127
  empower individuals, 100–101
  establishment of, 98, 100
  high-deductible plans and, 171–172
  promotion of, 50–51, 78–79, 159, 166
  pros and cons of, 172–175
  tax benefits of, 126, 172–173
  trends in use of, 137–138
Health-care expenditures
  affect of account-based plans on, 138–139
  consumer-driven care reduces, 81–92
  deductibility of, 49–52, 79, 101–102, 163
  increases in, 16, 18–19, 61
  on Medicaid, 113–114
  in U.S., 18, 142–143, 177

Healthcare Leadership Council (HLC), 194
Healthy choices, 166–167, 170–171
Healthy, Wealthy, and Wise (Hubbard et al.), 48, 125–126
Heriot, Gail, 56
Heritage Foundation, 195
Herrick, Devon M., 81
Herring, Robert, 152
Hertzberg, Hendrik, 129
High-deductible health plans (HDHPs), 86
  adverse selection and, 173
  are not effective, 120–122
  consumer-directed plans and, 134
  effects of, on quality and health, 136–137
  enrollees in, 138
  estimated cost benefits, 135–136
  HSAs and, 171–172
  individual choice and, 156–157
  lower costs, 96–99
  trends in use of, 137–138
  See also Consumer-driven health care
Holtz-Eakin, Douglas, 126
Home pregnancy tests, 88–89
Hoover Institution, 195
Hospitals
  competition among, 62–63
  local markets and, 67–68
  Medicare initiative, 69
House Joint Resolution 30, 27–31
HS Labs, 89
HSAs. *See* Health savings accounts (HSAs)
Hubbard, Allan B., 130, 132
Hubbard, R. Glenn, 48, 125–126

Human right
  health care as basic, 21–26, 32–34
  health care is not, 35–40
Hurricane Katrina, 111, 115–116

I

Income redistribution, 40
Individual responsibility. *See* Personal responsibility
Individualism, 157
Infant mortality, 18
Informed choice, 156
Institute for Health Freedom (IHF), 195
Institute for Medicine as a Profession, 74
International human rights, 23–25
Internet
  comparison shopping on, 91
  medical information on, 82–83, 85–88, 91–92, 98
Involuntary takings, 38–39

J

Jackson, Jesse L., Jr., 27
Jennings, Peter, 165, 166
Job mobility, 103
Johnson, Lyndon, 147
Johnson, Michele, 153
Jones, Jeffrey, 111

K

Kerry, John, 159
Kessler, Daniel, 48, 125–126
King, Judi, 169
Krugman, Paul, 123, 131
Kucinich, Dennis, 144

L

Leavitt, Mike, 116
Lee, Jason, 97–98
Legal costs, 54
Legal obstacles, to self-treatment, 92–95
Lesser, Cara S., 61
Liability, physician, 95
Liberal view
  of health care reform, 79–80, 157
  of right to health care, 21–22
  of U.S. health care system, 47
Libertarian view
  of health care reform, 78–79, 156–157
  of right to health care, 22
  of U.S. health care system, 46–47
Lieberman, Joe, 165
Lieberman, Trudy, 146
Life expectancy, 18
Local health care markets, 65–68
Locke, John, 39

M

Magnetic resonance imaging (MRI), 18
Maher, Walter, 181, 182, 183
Major, John, 42
Malpractice
  costs of, 74
  e-mail consultations and, 95
Managed care
  development of, 61, 62, 66
  distrust of insurers created by, 85
  failure of, 79
  lessons from, 70–71
Mandated health benefits, 107
Market solutions, 47

Market-based health care, problems with, 142–145, 179–181

Marshall, Jennifer A., 160

Mayo Clinic, 46

McDonald's, 181

McLachlin, Beverley, 42

Medicaid
administration of, 112–113
budget cuts to, 152–153
crisis in, 152–153
establishment of, 21, 78, 111–112
evolution of, 147–148
funding of, 112
Hurricane Katrina and, 115–117
privatization of, 153–154
restructuring of, 111–119
rising cost of, 64, 113–114
TennCare program and, 146–154
waste in, 109

Medical auction Web sites, 93–94

Medical boards, 92–93

Medical decisions
ill-informed, by consumers, 139–141
by individuals, 160–164

Medical expenses
bankruptcy from, 56–60, 178
deductibility of, 49–52, 79, 101–102, 126, 163
increases in, 18–19
routine care and, 127–128

Medical information
on Internet, 82–83, 85–88, 91–92, 98
need for, with CDHPs, 139–141
patient access to, 82–83
physician provided, 84–85

Medical marketplace, fallacy of, 132–133

Medical profession, 72–76, 74

Medical referrals, laws on, 93–94

Medical tests
costliness of, 18
patient-ordered, 88–90

Medicare
administrative costs of, 132, 184
for all Americans, 184–185
establishment of, 78
funding of, 112
initiatives of, 69
rates of reimbursement of, 53–54
rising cost of, 64
waste in, 109

Medicare Act of 2003, 97–98

Medicare Early Access Act, 185

MediKids, 185

MedlinePlus Web site, 87

Mexico, 21

Minneapolis (MN), 46

Minority groups, health outcomes of, 33

Minz, Morton, 176

Missouri Medicaid program, 152

Moffitt, Robert E., 160

Moral values, 161, 162

N

National Association of Manufacturers, 182

National Center for Policy Analysis (NCPA), 100, 102, 197

National Coalition on Health Care (NCHC), 197

National Health Service, 21

National Medical Association (NMA), 197–198

Natural law, 39

New Deal social programs, 78

O

Obesity, 165, 166
Online consultations, 87–88, 92
Over the counter (OTC) treatments, 90–91, 94
Oz, Mehmet, 73

P

Patients
    access to medical information, 82–83
    care management by, 86–92
    comparison shopping by, 91
    health care system endangers, 73
    increased self-care by, 98–99
    informed choice by, 156–157
    legal obstacles to self-care by, 92–95
    medical tests ordered by, 88–90
    neglect costs, 96–97
    physicians' relationships with, 84–85
    unwise decisions by, 127
Pay-for-performance (P4P) movement, 70–71
PepsiCo, 182
Personal responsibility
    health care and, 156–159, 165–171
    for medical decisions, 160–164
Physicians
    competition among, 62–63
    e-mail consultations with, 87–88, 95
    health care reform prescription and, 75–76
    liability and, 95
    licensing of, 92–93
    local market pressures and, 69
    online consultations with, 92

    patient care management by, 84–85
    professionalism of, 73
    services offered by, 66
    TennCare and, 151–152
Physicians for a National Health Program (PNHP), 198
Portable insurance, 102–103
Preferred Provider Organizations (PPOs), 86
Prescription drugs
    advertising, 83
    Bush plan for, 133
    comparison shopping for, 91
    regulations on, 94
President's Advisory Panel on Federal Tax Reform, 49
Preventive care, 33, 137
Pricing structure, government-regulated, 53–55
Privatized health care
    in Canada, 41–42
    in England, 43
    in Europe, 43–44
Product prices, health-care costs and, 16–17
Profits, 184
Project EINO (Everybody In, Nobody Out), 198–199
Providers
    health care system endangers, 73
    See also Physicians

Q

Quality of care, effects of HDHPs on, 136–137
Quest Diagnostics, 89
QuesTest.com, 89

R

RAND Corporation, 16, 134, 135, 199

Reagan, Ronald, 158

Referrals, laws on, 93–94

Regulations. *See* Government regulations

Relman, Arnold, 142, 143, 144

Roosevelt, Franklin D., 23, 25

Rothman, David, 74

Routine care, 127–128

Rx-to-OTC switching, 94

S

Schiavo, Terri, 147

Screening tests, 89–90

Scullt, Thomas, 113

Second Bill of Rights, 23, 25

Self-diagnostic tests, 88–90

Self-treatment
  for chronic conditions, 104
  legal obstacles to, 92–95
  lowers costs, 90–91
  shift toward, 98–99

Single-payer system
  benefits business, 176–183
  proponents of, 22
  See also Universal health care

Smith, Grace V., 160

Smith, Lori, 147

Socialized medicine, 26, 41–44, 158–159

Soumerai, Stephen, 151

Specialty services, competition for, 66

St. Goran's Hospital (Stockholm), 44

Starbucks, 184

Stark, Pete, 184

State medical licensing, 92–93

States, role of, in providing health care, 21

Sundquist, Don, 148–149, 152–153

Supermarket industry, 177–178

Supreme Court of Canada, 41, 43

Sweden, 43–44

T

Tax benefits, of HSAs, 172–173

Tax code reform, 48–52, 79, 101–102, 163

TennCare program, 146–154

Third-party payer system
  increase costs, 96–97
  personal decision-making and, 160–164

Tiered-benefit plans, 134–135

Tollen, Laura, 98

Tort reform, 107, 108

Treatment options, expansion of, 83

U

Uninsured persons
  difficulties of, 32
  increases in, 46, 176–177
  statistics on, 17–18, 24, 30, 61, 143, 184

Unions, 17, 178–179

United Food and Commercial Workers (UFCW) union, 178

United Nations, 21, 23

United Neighborhood Health Services (UNHS), 150

United States
  health care spending in, as percent of GDP, 132, 142–143, 177

lack of government-sponsored health care in, 16–18, 21
per person health-care costs in, 18
U.S. Chamber of Commerce, 182
U.S. Constitution, health care amendment to, 27–31
U.S. health care system
administrative costs of, 132
crisis in, 24
debate over, 46–47
deregulation of, 53–55
endangers patients and providers, 72–76
evolution of, 78
failures of, 61–65
fragmented nature of, 131
local level of, 65–68
market models do not apply to, 142–145
ranking of, 30
tax code reform and, 48–52
Universal Declaration of Human Rights, 21, 23
Universal health care
benefits business, 176
decline in, 41–44
funding of, 29–31
lack of, in U.S., 16–18, 21
Medicare as model for, 185
mobilization of support for, 25–26
United States should provide, 23–26

Urban Institute, 199

V

Values-driven reform, 160–164
Virtual exams, 89–90

W

Wagoner, G. Richard, Jr., 183
Waiting lists, for health care in Canada, 41–42
Walker, David, 177
Wal-Mart, 124, 178
Web sites, medical auction, 93–94
See also Internet
Wells, Paul, 123
Werntz, Raymond, 179
William, Walter E., 38
Wood, Diane, 150–151
Woolhandler, Steffie, 59, 60
Wootan, Margo, 166
Worker's compensation insurance, 176
World Health Organization (WHO), 30
World War II, 17

Y

Young adults, uninsured, 17–18

Z

Zaidi, Sarah, 23